IT'S A DON'S LIFE

Also by Mary Beard

Pompeii: The Life of a Roman Town
The Parthenon
The Colosseum (with Keith Hopkins)
The Roman Triumph

IT'S A DON'S LIFE

Mary Beard

PROFILE BOOKS

First published in Great Britain in 2009 by
PROFILE BOOKS LTD
3A Exmouth House
Pine Street
London EC1R 0JH
www.profilebooks.com

10 9 8 7 6 5 4 3 2 1

Typeset in Minion by MacGuru Ltd
info@macguru.org.uk
Printed and bound in Great Britain by
CPI Bookmarque Ltd, Croydon, Surrey

A CIP catalogue record for this book is available from the British Library.

ISBN 978 1 84668 251 3
eISBN 978 1 84765 246 1

For Tony Francis, Xjy, Michael Bulley, Anthony Alcock, Richard, Paul Potts, SW Foska, PL, Jackie, Lord Truth (Ronald Rogers), Jane, Oliver Nicholson, Lucy, Eileen, FG, Arindam Bandyopadhaya, Lidwina, Monica, Nicholas Wibberley, Richard Baron, David Kirwan, Bingley, Simone, Steve the Neighbour and all my other friends on the blog.

Illustration Credits

p. 5   Antinous Mondragone: Courtesy Musée du Louvre, Paris. Photo RMN Hervé Lewandowski.
p. 86   Ladies toilet sign. Photo by Debbie Whittaker.
p. 180   Claudius and Britannia panel: Courtesy New York University Excavations at Aphrodisias. Photo by Guido Petruccioli.
p. 214   Bust of Julius Caesar. Photo by Boris Horvat. AFP/Getty Images.
p. 230   Disappointing ruins. Taken from *Signs of Life* (Harper Collins, 2005). Photo by Dave Askwith.

*

While every effort has been made to contact the authors of comments quoted and copyright holders, the author and publishers would be grateful for information about any they have been unable to trace.

Introduction

A don's life is enormously rewarding – and fun. I can think of few better ways of earning a living. It is also hard work, frustrating, and all too often misrepresented. In the absence of any other news, a desperate journalist can always fall back on taking a pot shot at the three-month summer holidays we dons are supposed to enjoy, or on whipping up outrage about the 'unfair' selection procedures of Oxford and Cambridge in particular. Do we really only let in those kids who can tell their sherry from their port, or have been trained to cope with our impenetrable – and, frankly, mad – questions?

Since April 2006, my blog – *A Don's Life* – has shared some of the day-to-day realities of working in a university, and tried to quash a few myths. No, the summer vacation is not a 'holiday'. You won't find us on the golf course or the beach (unless we are working on seashore beetles, that is). And no, we don't dream up interview questions about what it would feel like to be a light bulb or a strawberry, just to trip up the unwary (see p. 249 for the inside story).

Of course, Cambridge is not a 'typical' university. There's probably no such thing. I've worked in three, in Britain and the US, and each one has been very different. All the same, I'm sure that many of the themes of *A Don's Life* would be recognisable in any university, anywhere in the world (take a look at the 'willy waving' on p. 100).

I'm also a classicist – a species far less endangered than you have no doubt been led to believe. The blog tries to capture something of the pleasure, and the point, of studying the Greeks and Romans: from ancient Roman jokes (p. 183) to the discovery of a battered statue from the river Rhône, which may (or, more likely, may not) be a portrait of Julius Caesar (p. 214).

The posts included in this book are published more or less as they appeared on the blog – with only the occasional explanation added, spelling mistakes corrected and (regular readers of *A Don's Life* will be relieved to learn) apostrophes inserted where required. You can dip into them in any order. But there *is* a narrative that runs from start to finish, from my very first tentative post 'Pink or purple' to the semi-professional blogger at the end.

I suspect that, over all, the blog makes my life seem more exciting and action-packed than it really is. I've tried to capture the flavour of an average day (p. 163). But in general there is not much 'blog-worthy' about an evening spent marking fifteen essays on the run-up to the Peloponnesian War (fascinating a subject as it is), nor about a morning in the library failing to find that crucial reference in Cicero (or was it Livy?) that you've lost.

And it's not easy to share all those hours spent teaching the students and thinking about how they are getting on. After all, no undergraduate wants to find the failings of their latest essay or exam discussed with the rest of the world on the web. No doctoral student wants to see the latest chapter of their thesis publicly dissected. Do bear this in mind as you read – and turn to the essay at the end of the book for further more leisurely reflections on the 'blogosphere'.

You will also find here a growing relationship with a wonderful group of commenters. The comments on many blogs are little short of abusive rants. Not so those on *A Don's Life*, which often reflect with wit, learning and experience on the subject at issue, whether it be the bones of St Cuthbert, David Beckham's new tattoo or the real identity of that statue pulled from the Rhône. Some of my favourite comments are included here, as they appeared on the blog (occasionally shortened, but not edited in any other way).

I am tremendously grateful to all those commenters who gave permission for their comments to be reprinted. It is to those who have commented most often over the years that this book-of-the-blog is dedicated.

*

You can find, and comment on, my blog at:
http://timesonline.typepad.com/dons_life

Pink or purple?

25 April 2006

Our undergraduates trooped back to college this weekend to be greeted by a big poster explaining how they could 'find their seat'. Not helpful advice from the housekeeping department. But timely information from the University examinations office to all those students who apparently don't know where their exams are held, and don't know where to sit even if they do.

Easter term in Cambridge is all about exams. Intellectual ambitions get traded in for an anxious diet of revision, morale boosting and what used (before it was banned) to be called 'hand-holding'. We give parties to take their young minds off it, supervisions to put them back on again. And more advice is asked for and given than even the biggest swot could take in.

In the old days we could escape a bit, by locking ourselves in our rooms and putting 'OUT' on the door. But now emails get you any time of day or night – sillier as the term wears on. 'Dear Professor Beard, Hope you don't mind me asking but is it OK to write in pink fibre tip, or would purple be better …?' as one emailed me last year. (Answer: Try black/What do you think?/No, I don't think you'll fail …).

And when the day of reckoning arrives, we're all so keen for our charges to succeed that we turn ourselves into an unpaid taxi service. Any morning in the second half of May, you'll find the same touching scene repeated all over Cambridge: a tutor driving to the exam room at top speed, transporting some burly young lad with a handsome golden hello from

McKinsey's already in the bag – all because his alarm clock didn't go off, or he was hung over, or he'd forgotten where his seat was. (In every other university in the country, I should say – except probably Oxford – getting yourself to the paper on time is thought to be part of the test.)

So is it all worth it? Some of us, given half a chance, would simply scrap the lot. 'Continuous assessment' would look more humane and it may well be fairer to women (who, across the board, don't do as well as men on the current system). And it certainly wouldn't take such a ridiculous amount of time and energy all round – which is in danger of seeming out of proportion when some 70% of these kids will now get a 2.1 in their final exams anyway.

For better or worse, grade inflation or superior student effort, gone are the days of the 'gentleman's third'; thirds are now the human tragedies. And I've even heard it, half-seriously, suggested that we should just give them all a 2.1 as a matter of course, and that exams should only be for those who wanted to 'bid for a first'. That would certainly cut down the labour.

But I can't help thinking that there's life in the old system yet. For a start, no problem with plagiarism. Unlike with 'assessed essays', done in their own time, you don't have to type every suspiciously clever phrase into Google to find out where it might have come from.

Anonymity, too, is a good protection all round. We don't actually know who wrote the scripts we are marking (and, as they now word-process all their term work, we don't even recognise their handwriting like we used to). While they don't have much clue who on our side is marking them – certainly not enough of a clue to be able to take the American option of sending their parents or lawyers into your office, or in the worst case appearing with a gun to demand higher grades.

And having lived through GSCE and A level course work at home, I can't imagine I'm the only one to think that 'continuous assessment' might be a lot more painful than this old-fashioned form of 'sudden death'. Just stress all the year round.

So here we go ... only eight weeks and it's all over.

Sex in the sculpture garden

25 May 2006

The traces were undeniable. We were peering at one of
the most famous Roman portrait sculptures in the world,
discussing with art-historical intensity the provenance, the
marble and the tooling. Then someone had the nerve to point
out that on its cheek and its chin were the faint but clear marks
of two bright red lipstick kisses.

The sculpture in question was the colossal head – known as
the 'Mondragone Head' – of Antinous the young lover of the
emperor Hadrian, who died mysteriously, Robert-Maxwell-
style, in AD 130 after falling into the river Nile. So distraught
was the bereaved emperor that he flooded the Roman world
with statues of his beloved, made him a god and named a
city after him. There are more surviving statues of Antinous
than of almost any other character in antiquity (many from
Hadrian's own villa at Tivoli). They all share the same sultry
sensuousness and the luscious pouting lips that characterise
the 'Mondragone'.

His usual home is in the Louvre, where he ended up in
1808, courtesy of Napoleon. But we were in Leeds, where he
has come to be star of an exquisite show at the Henry Moore
Institute which opened today. This has drawn together 14 of
the many Antinous images, a little gallery of beautiful boys
who have travelled from Dresden, Athens, Rome, Cambridge
and elsewhere. One of the show's themes – appropriately
enough – is the question of what makes a statue, or a body,
desirable. What is it to 'want' a work of art?

The erotic charm of sculpture has a long literary history. Back in the second century AD, the Greek satirist Lucian told the story of one young obsessive who contrived to get locked up at night with Praxiteles' famous statue of Aphrodite at Cnidus. The young man went mad; but the indelible stain on the statue's thigh was proof enough of what had gone on. Oscar Wilde picked up the theme in his 'Charmides' – an engaging piece of doggerel, in which the hero smuggles himself into the Parthenon and 'paddles' up to Athena's statue.

Until today I had never quite imagined that this was anything other than a literary conceit. But the evidence was before my eyes.

The assault on the 'Mondragone' certainly did not happen in Leeds. The curators there were as gobsmacked as anyone to discover the tell-tale marks. But at some point between Paris and its unpacking at the Henry Moore, some latter-day Hadrian – man or woman – had given it a couple of real red smackers. In jest, in irony or in passion, we shall probably never know.

It couldn't have happened to a more appropriate work of art than this surrogate of imperial desire. Presumably it's much what the emperor Hadrian himself had in mind.

Big Brother at uni

6 June 2006

Living in a student ghetto in a student city can make you feel horribly middle-aged. It's not so much their extravagant – or extravagantly revealing – clothing, that you could no longer get away with yourself. Actually I rather like the annual summer display of belly buttons down King's Parade. And it's not their youthful argot either. Even I find myself saying 'uni', when I mean 'university'.

What is most dispiriting for us old liberals is more ideological. It's the way the students have come to take for granted all the things we fought against and lost. They can't imagine what life would be like with a nationalised railway or free eye-tests; and they can't think what a second post would actually be for.

But even more alarming is that most of them have entirely bought into the idea of a surveillance culture. Show them a gloomy bike shed, a leafy path or a picturesque bend in the river, and there is nothing that your average Cambridge undergraduate would like to do more than install a CCTV camera in it.

They say it makes them feel safer. And I suppose that you can't entirely blame them for not bucking the general trend. Ever since that macabre CCTV image of a pair of kids walking off with a toddler set the police on to the killers of Jamie Bulger, CCTV has had a peculiarly unchallengeable status among the British public as a crime detection or even prevention device.

Whether it is really effective or not is quite another matter. When my own faculty was broken into for the usual haul of laptops and data-projectors a few months ago, the police didn't even bother to look at what might have been recorded by the camera trained directly at the front door. 'Wouldn't be a good enough image, luv.'

All the same, the majority of the population is, I suspect, rather proud that we have more CCTV cameras per head than any other country in the world – even though a glance at most foreign newspapers suggests that, from the outside, it looks like a very odd enthusiasm for a liberal democracy.

And it's on those civil liberties grounds that I have always found the students' embracing of CCTV such a puzzle. I wouldn't mind it if they said, 'Look, we know what the libertarian arguments are, but on balance we think that it's worth the risk.' But in fact these highly intelligent young people (and half of them Amnesty members) just look blank when some old grey beard like me warns darkly about the dangers of surveillance. If anything, they'll mutter the stupid mantra that you have nothing to fear if you've done no wrong. How could this be?

I was beginning to blame the usual suspects – viz. they must have been taught this at school – when confirmation of these suspicions arrived by an unexpected domestic route. My son appeared at home, just before some big exams, having lost his backpack with all his notes. He seemed remarkably insouciant. (I wasn't.) But sure enough the next day he came home, the backpack found.

What he had done was go to the school CCTV controller clutching his school timetable – and so he could be tracked through the day. There he was entering the French lesson with the backpack, and here he was coming out of it without. Hey presto, it was found in the French room.

This, I realised, must be a wizard procedure repeated over and over again in schools throughout the country, as disorganised adolescents get re-united with belongings thanks to the CCTV cameras. If Big Brother has always helped you find your lost property, no wonder you have a softer spot for him than I do.

Tampons for Africa

13 June 2006

I do have a soft spot for *Woman's Hour*. I like the way it
squeezes in wonderfully subversive feminist reports next to
those drearily wholesome recipes for tuna pasta bake. And I
have a particularly soft spot for it at the moment because one
of the current producers is the inestimable Victoria Brignell.
Victoria did Classics at Cambridge a few years ago, was
clever and sparky, moved on to the BBC – and happens to be
quadriplegic.

But, uncharacteristically, on Monday they missed a trick
with a pious little item on sanitary protection in Kenya.

It was indeed tear-jerking stuff. There were interviews with
young girls who missed school, even dropped out of education
entirely, because they didn't have pads. They couldn't bear, they
said, to go to school with blood on their clothes. So there's a
campaign – backed by NGOs and Kenyan women MPs – to get
sanpro (as the trade calls it) given out free in schools, and to
get the world's women to donate their surplus.

To start with, it all sounded pretty compelling. But soon
it was clear that a lot of questions were going to remain
unanswered. What, for example, did the women of Kenya do
before the prospect of Western sanpro was trailed before them?
There were a few dark references to dung and lack of hygiene.
And my mind raced to the idea of menstrual exclusion and
the wonderful prospect of women all menstruating in the
menstrual hut together, doing their school work and having
a great time – until some well-meaning anthropologist came

and told them they shouldn't buy into these ideas of pollution. Who knows?

In this case it was hard to resist the conclusion that they might once have had some reasonably effective local method of dealing with the bleeding. But now these poor girls were sitting there worrying about making a mess on their skirts – and waiting for a supply of commercial pads that would never quite meet the demand.

More to the point – who is actually making this sanpro for Kenya? Was the campaign looking to build local, and locally owned, pad factories? Or to develop hygienic, reusable and eco-friendly methods? No, the idea seemed to be that we should airlift in the products of the great multinational companies, who already make a mint out of menstruating first-world women.

A quick trawl of the web shows that the business world has already spotted the African continent as a burgeoning market for top price sanpro. It recognises that there is a certain difficulty in 'enlarging the consumer base' and that 'lower income groups are less likely to purchase sanitary protection' (a market research triumph, for sure). But then, if you can get us to buy it and donate, you've made the profit anyway.

The case of Zimbabwe is horribly instructive, There is a pad crisis there, too. Why? Because Johnson & Johnson moved out of the country in 1999 when the economic going got rough and they have been forced to import from South Africa.

I thought that we had learned from the 'baby formula for Africa' débâcle. But, even if on a smaller scale, this looks like much the same story.

Comments

Mary, your 'menstrual hut' fantasy might have been fine 100 years ago but we're talking about modern girls going to contemporary secondary schools trying to get a professional education. The idea that these aspirations have been foisted upon Kenyan girls by 'anthropologists' is insulting. We're not talking about girls sitting round in villages grinding mealies while their menfolk hunt lions. These are girls who have to take the crowded public mini-bus to school, who wear uniform as they walk down city streets just like the girls you see in Cambridge ... Oh, and I wouldn't describe myself as a subversive feminist. I'm an African man.

BOMAN'GOMBE

Mixed messages?

16 June 2006

The dust has quickly died down after St Hilda's announced ten days ago that it would be admitting men. The last 'all-girls' college in Oxford (as most reports patronisingly put it) finally relented and opened its doors.

I wasn't exactly thrilled by the news. There could after all be a knock-on effect on my own cherished single-sex Cambridge college. And besides, it was hard to follow the logic of why letting men into St Hilda's would improve the educational opportunities of women.

But worse were the arguments that came out on either side of this debate. 'Pro-mixers' tended to heave a sigh of relief that this quaint anachronism had at last been done away with. The supporters of single-sex colleges, I'm afraid, did little better. Here, they said, was a place where women could be cherished outside the nasty, competitive hurly-burly of a man's world.

Wrong on both counts. Women's colleges are not havens of refuge for those that can't hack it in mixed company. And as for the accusation of anachronism – they are probably better equipped for promoting women's opportunities into the twenty-first century than most other institutions.

This isn't the place for the PR about why my college offers a marvellous opportunity for clever women. Enough to say that it serves its students well because it is part of the wider university community, not a refuge from it.

Most good teachers advising their sixth-form students have got this message. It's only occasionally now that I visit a school, chat amiably to some engagingly articulate and forthcoming potential applicants to Cambridge and then find my eye drawn to a solitary soul in the corner – well-scrubbed, dressed in sub-Laura Ashley and quiet as a mouse. 'That's Deirdre,' says the teacher. 'She's thinking of applying to Newnham.'

True, Deirdre may turn out to be really smart underneath (especially when she's escaped from the orbit of her more self-confident but less clever classmates). But you see what I mean.

So why support women's colleges? Aside from all the advantages for undergraduates, there are some very solid institutional reasons. The idea that women's colleges are a strange Victorian anachronism, while the rest of the university is 'gender normal', is frankly bonkers.

For most of its 800 years, Cambridge University has been a 'boys' institution. Women only got degrees here after World War II (they took the exams much earlier, but didn't get the piece of paper). Now there is a huge and sincere campaign to change this – but there's also centuries of history to work against. Look around the portraits hanging in any college dining hall. With the exception of the occasional matriarch benefactor of the sixteenth century, they are all men.

The raw data are themselves an indication of the current problem. The latest 'Equality and Diversity' progress report records that there are just 46 women professors in the university, as against 404 men. To be fair, that was an increase of nine women professors on the previous year – but then again the number of women 'Readers', the next rank down, fell by two. To put it in an entirely personal way, for many of my 20 something years as a University teacher in Cambridge I was the only woman lecturer in a Faculty of about 30 men.

The University is certainly on the case. My own heart sinks at some of its initiatives. The idea that there should be at least two women on every University committee is a noble gesture, but it presages a lifetime of administration for me, while (some of) my male colleagues are let off the hook and get some thinking time in the library. What we really need is a place within the university where women are not just present in single figures but have a critical mass – and that is, of course, the women's colleges.

Until things change, most women teachers at Cambridge are likely to be ambivalent about their careers. I have found it a wonderful place to work (otherwise I wouldn't have stayed). But, like all of us, I bear the scars of a bloke-ish institution.

My favourite (and somewhat self-inflicted) scar is this – and it must be typical of many women's experience here.

When I was pregnant with child number one, I was the 'meetings secretary' of the University classical society, the Cambridge Philological Society. This involved attending meetings three times a term and, in Victorian style, reading out the minutes of the last meeting. ('Professor X read a paper on "The digamma in archaic poetry"' or whatever). With ludicrous heroism, and loathsome self-advertisement, I turned out to do this chore less than a week after the baby was born. Never was I going to let the guys say that giving birth interfered with duties to my subject.

For the next term or two, I went on with the job. But at the end of a teaching afternoon (the meetings started at 4.30) I needed desperately, and uncomfortably, to go home and feed the baby. So I would read the minutes and, once the lecture had begun, I would slip away.

Ten years later, I had long resigned the 'meetings secretary' role, and they were looking for a new candidate to fill the post.

'It's a drag,' I said to one of my colleagues. 'You have to turn up for every meeting.'

'Ah,' he said. 'You were the lazy one who used to walk out before the lecture had even finished.'

I had got no kudos at all. Quite the reverse.

It had been pointless heroism on my part. But the jibe would never have happened at Newnham.

Comments

In the physics department of my undergraduate university, the door of the ground-floor women's toilet had clearly read 'MAIDS' at some point in the past. The actual label had been removed, but its shadow remained etched into the faded wood. I've come to think of this gone-but-not-forgotten sign as a metaphor for the progress women have made in academia over the past few decades ... The corresponding men's toilet, by the way, was located directly opposite the mechanical workshop, and was labelled 'REAL MEN'.

AARDVARK

Is Latin too hard?

28 June 2006

Research at Durham University claims to show kids are put off taking Latin GCSE because it is too hard – about a grade harder than other supposedly 'hard' subjects. That is to say, if you can get a grade C at Latin, you'd be in the running for a B in Physics or German. And teachers, it's said, have too much of an eye on the league tables to persuade their pupils to take the risk.

At least this is a change from the usual story about Latin. More than a third of all takers get the top A* grade (compared with less than 4% in Business Studies and around 6% in German – or, going the other way, 55% in Greek). And 60% in Latin get A* and A combined. How easy it must be, some wonder.

Actually, these stories are easily compatible. Latin is an extremely self-selecting subject, chosen by some of our very brightest kids. No wonder they do extremely well – and, as I see when they apply to us, often get a string of other very high grades. The question is, should Latin be the subject of choice for the less bright, too?

People – we classicists included – sometimes get in a muddle here. There is no question at all that Latin and Greek should be available to the talented of whatever wealth and class. The erosion of Classics in the maintained sector is a disgrace in Britain and elsewhere. But is it actually a sensible educational goal to try to spread Latin and Greek right across the ability range?

There's a baby-and-bathwater problem here. At the moment Latin and Greek are the only foreign language GCSEs where you still read some literature in the original language. Thank heavens that OCR, the only exam board now offering classical languages, has valiantly kept on the 'set books', so some 16-year-olds still get more than a taste of real Virgil, Catullus or Homer. Sure, it's difficult – but interesting, too, and it's keeping some of our brightest-and-best engaged and on-message. You could notch it all down a level, but only at a cost. A simplified GCSE (with simplified Virgil) would not offer the same stimulus at all.

But there is in fact a bigger point here. What do we think that studying any of these subjects at GSCE is FOR? In modern languages, the repetitive, multiple-choice tests on how to find the cathedral from the car park, or how to order a pizza in Bologna are mind-numbing for the bright; but they do fulfil a function. Anyone might need to order a meal or ask directions in a foreign city. If GCSE promotes that skill, so much the better – despite the doomladen prophets of dumbing down.

Why then learn Latin? Certainly not for conversation. And not – at GCSE level, at least – just to learn about the ancient world (there's an excellent Classical Civilisation exam for that). Nor to learn formal grammar (which can be taught more economically in a myriad of other ways). The central point of learning Latin is to be able to read some of the extraordinary literature written a couple of millennia ago. It can be formidably hard. Asking a school student to read Tacitus is a bit like asking an English learner to go off and read *Finnegans Wake*. But it is what makes the whole enterprise intellectually worthwhile. Make the whole thing easier (up the multiple choice and downplay the real literature) and you've removed the very point of learning the language in the first place.

And that's what's going to kill the subject.

Comments

Latin is anything but a 'dead language'. For several decades
Finnish radio has been broadcasting the news in Latin. They have
even recorded Elvis Presley songs in the language.

Nuntii Latini – 'News in Latin' – is a weekly review of world
news in classical Latin, the only international broadcast of its kind
in the world, produced by YLE, the Finnish Broadcasting Company
...

So you see, Tacitus rides on ... the airwaves. Just tune in and
listen and learn.

PETER ATHEY

Does Latin 'train the brain'?

10 July 2006

Correspondents to *The Times* have been exercised over the value of a 'classical education', so I am returning to the topic. What IS the point of learning Latin?

There are several reasons often touted that seem to me wide of the mark. (Sorry – a typically academic way to kick off; but these do have to be disposed of first.)

You do NOT learn Latin because it helps you to understand the spells in Harry Potter, or to read the slogans on pound coins. That may be a side benefit, but frankly you're not missing much in life if you don't get all of Harry's wizardry.

You do NOT learn Latin because it helps you learn other languages. Again that may be a knock-on effect. But if you want to learn (say) Spanish, it's better to get on with it, not learn Latin first to make it easier. (Besides, I always feel that any subject that tries to justify itself by claiming that it helps you learn something else is on the way out.)

You do NOT learn Latin because it hones your critical and logical thinking. True, I rather like the jingle cited in one *Times* letter that 'Latin trains the brain' (just as I am touched by another plaudit for the sheer uselessness of the language). But Latin is only one of many subjects that does this. If we gave our kids three lessons in formal logic each week, we'd probably soon notice a difference in their critical power.

No, you learn Latin because of what was written in it – and because of the direct access that Latin gives you to a literary tradition that lies at the very heart (not just at the root) of Western culture.

Virgil's *Aeneid* and Tacitus' *Annals* (to name only two) are as mind-opening and life-changing works of literature as *Hamlet*, *Paradise Lost* or *Anna Karenina*. It is worth learning Latin just to be able to read them.

But more than that, the Latin classics are so embedded in the Western literary tradition that as a culture (I'm not necessarily talking about individual readers here) we would be lost in our own world if we could not access them. What would we make of Dante or Milton, for example, if we could not read them side by side with Virgil? (For that matter, I'm always amazed that modern historians seem happy to work on figures such as Gladstone when they don't know a word of the classical languages that were his daily bread and butter.)

Won't translations do? Up to a point, yes. And let's be honest, most people in this country for the last 500 years or so have consumed their Latin literature in the vernacular. Like it or not, Latin has always been an élite subject. But translations aren't a complete substitute, for two reasons.

First, if we let Latin drop entirely, who is going to be able to understand all the 'new' Latin that continues to be discovered by the page, if not the volume-full – much of it (like the Vindolanda letters) from Britain? Or are we going to keep a handful of boffins on the job, translating the new stuff as it appears?

Second, translations never quite get you to the real thing. They are always versions, recast for whatever audience, time or place they have in mind. Try picking up any Victorian translation of Virgil and ask yourself if the *Aeneid* would still be read today if that was the only version we had. Literature can't survive in translation alone.

Ask a silly question

13 July 2006

Last week I spent a morning doing 'media training', a marvellous crash course that the university occasionally lays on for its staff. The idea is to make you a more 'effective communicator' on radio and television.

About half the morning was theory (what to wear, how to prepare, when and how to smile, etc.). The other half was practical, and took the form of some recorded interviews, which you then went over – and picked to pieces – with instructors and fellow victims. It was humiliating, but extraordinarily helpful. 'Where's your killer point?' the instructor asked after we'd listened to me discussing the benefits of Latin. A fair cop, I thought. There wasn't one.

I don't imagine that I shall be following all the rules we were given. Honestly, I can't see me in the recommended pastel colours and trim jackets, even if they are flattering in front of the camera. But, at the very least, it's nice to know what the rules are that you're breaking.

Overall, the main point seemed to be that you would do a better media interview once you had learned how to 'set the agenda'. Roughly translated this means 'how not to answer the question'.

Academics, it seems, are very bad at not answering the question. A big part of our day job involves explaining to students why 'irrelevance will be penalised' (as is blazoned across many Cambridge exam papers) and trying to convince the younger generation that academic success usually goes to those who answer the question that is set – not the question they would like to have been asked.

The result is that your average don will obediently wrestle with even the stupidest questions posed by the most ill-informed interviewers, while the minutes for moving on to more interesting territory tick speedily away. I've often enough gone down the primrose path of 'So what kind of dog breeds did the Romans have, then … ?' (search me – nasty ones, I think), when we should have been discussing the intriguing power of ancient mythical monsters.

It was good to learn some tactics for dealing with this. And ever since I've been practising in my head phrases like 'That's an interesting question, but I think the really important point is …' or 'Yes, but we first need to think about …'

But our group did begin to have some qualms about the future of radio discussion if every participant came along with their own agenda already set and ready to plug it at all costs. It would turn a programme like *Nightwaves* (never mind *In Our Time*) from frank and friendly discussion into a series of monologues. And anyway, when you're a radio listener rather than performer, don't you just hate the guys who won't answer the question?

Whether I've actually got any better at 'effective communication', I'll have to wait and see. I did give some of my newfound skills a trial run yesterday, when I was interviewed for an enterprising BBC 4 programme on the image of the Romans on television. This is set to coincide with a summer repeat of the 1976 BBC series of *I Claudius* – and, classicists note, with any luck it will include an unmissable clip of Mortimer Wheeler in 1960, pondering on the similarities of the British and Roman empires, while puffing on his pipe on some temple steps.

I fear, once more, that I broke several of the rules. Where was the jacket? And alcohol (a predictable no-no) had been consumed in sufficient quantities at a party the night before that the killer points didn't come easy. But perhaps I have managed to correct that distracting little slant of the head. I can hardly wait to watch.

What are academics for?

18 July 2006

Because we have very few fixed hours of work, university teachers are often assumed to have loads of free time. People see us taking retail therapy on a Tuesday morning or having a long lunch, and they tend to forget that all our weekend and most of the night was spent in the library. Not great for family life, as most partners of academics complain.

This makes us easy prey to all kinds of demands from those who think that we can easily give some of that 'free time' to them. There are scores of 'independent television makers' who will ring you up and try to get you to plan their new programme on gladiators, sex in the ancient world, the fall of the Roman empire, or whatever, over the phone. Now that email is the standard medium of communication, we've got out of practice at the old art of putting the receiver down – which is, of course, why they ring.

Then there are the eager sixth-formers who think that an enthusiastic letter or email will prompt you to give them more help with their A level course work than you should by rights offer. As I can testify, there are more kids in this country working on 'Roman Women' than you could possibly believe.

It is presumably in response to this kind of pressure that a senior Oxford academic has published on the web his, punningly titled, 'Rules of Engagement', for anyone wanting to use his services.

These rules consist mostly of a list of things he won't do:

'No external lectures/conference papers will be given in term time. Only exceptionally will lectures/conference papers be given outside term.'

'No books or articles will be read for publishers in advance of publication.'

'No meeting in London starting before 11.00 a.m. or 11.30 on Mondays unless overnight stay is funded.'

But there are other canny conditions laid down:

'All travel should be refunded within 6 weeks of the journey undertaken. Thereafter interest will be charged at a rate equivalent to that on my credit card. All air journeys lasting over two and a half hours will be expected to be funded at business-class level.'

'Books will be reviewed for journals, etc. only exceptionally, and only if they are major reviews of substantial length with a notice of at least 8 weeks.'

I can see where he is coming from. I still get angry about some universities abroad who have taken more than six months to refund my travel expenses. And certainly there have been times when rearranging my university teaching, taking a cold and uncomfortable train journey cross-country and then talking to a handful of conscripts in a village hall has not quite seemed worth the trouble it has caused.

But what has happened to the idea of public responsibility? The fact that academics get paid (albeit inadequately) by the state surely gives them a duty to the community more widely. It may not be part of our contracts, but it is certainly part of how most of us understand the job in its widest sense, to spread our word outside the academy. Draughty church halls, lectures in unglamorous locations with no travel expenses (prisons are one of my particular favourites), short reviews in local papers all have their place on the agenda.

Most important of all are the talks to schools (strikingly absent from the 'Rules of Engagement'). True, these are not lucrative and they aren't always exactly fun. It isn't easy for the untrained to hold the attention of 60 or so 14-year-olds, especially when half the audience has been dragooned into your talk to give their exhausted teacher an hour off. But somewhere in there, just occasionally, is someone whose horizons you might change.

The husband, now an art historian, recounts just such an eye-opening moment from his own school days. He had never thought of art history as a subject you might actually study, until Nikolaus Pevsner came to his school and gave a still-remembered talk on local buildings, and – in particular – on the different architectural histories of the towns of Bristol and Bath. Cliché as it must seem, it was the start of another art-historical career.

Pevsner was already a well-established figure at that point. But I rather doubt that he laid down careful conditions about his travel expenses and his credit card bill.

They make a desert and call it peace

24 July 2006

I am usually suspicious of claims that understanding the history of the ancient world helps you understand the history of our own. When people tell me that antiquity was so like today, I tend to object that it was actually very different in almost every possible respect.

But two of the topics in Roman history that I regularly teach have recently come to seem almost uncomfortably topical – and raw.

The first is the whole theme of 'native' resistance to the Roman empire. If you didn't have the military resources, how could you stand up against the ancient world's only superpower?

Between the third century BC and the first century AD, Rome systematically extended its control over the world from the Sahara to Scotland. As with most empires, it was not without its advantages for at least some of the conquered. I'm not just talking about consumer goods, literacy, water and drains (which didn't impact on as much of the Roman world as we often fondly imagine). Rome's imperial strategy was first to incorporate the local élites and then gradually spread citizenship, with all its advantages, throughout its whole territory. It was generosity, even if sprung from self-interest.

That said, what could you do if you didn't fancy being taken over by Rome, having your self-determination removed and being forced to sing to the Roman tune (as well as pay Roman taxes)? The Roman legions represented an insuperable military force. In pitched battle they might occasionally be delayed (if you could muster vast numbers of forces while the Romans themselves were off guard), but while their power was at its height they could not be defeated.

Barbarians were not stupid. They did not pointlessly waste their men's lives in formal battle lines against the superpower. Instead they did what the disadvantaged will always do against overwhelming military odds: they ignored the rules of war and resorted to guerrilla tactics, trickery and terrorism.

Much of this was ghastly and cruel. Our image of plucky little Asterix with his boy-scoutish japes against the Roman occupation is about as true to life as a cartoon strip would be that made suicide bombing seem like fun. Boudicca's scythed chariots (if they ever existed) were the ancient equivalent of car bombs. In terrorising the occupying forces she was said to have had the breasts slashed off the Roman civilian women and sewn into their mouths.

Roman writers were outraged at barbarian tactics in war, decried their illegal weapons and their flouting of military law. (In fact 'terrorist' sometimes captures the Roman sense of the Latin word *barbarus* better than the more obvious 'barbarian'.) But in the face of invincible imperialism, they must have felt they were using the only option they had. Does it sound familiar?

My second teaching topic is the famous account by the Roman historian Tacitus of the career of his father-in-law, Agricola, who was governor of Britain in the late first century AD and extended Roman power north into Scotland. On one occasion the barbarians were foolish enough to risk a pitched battle – and, just before it, Tacitus puts into the mouth of the British leader, Calgacus, a rousing speech denouncing not only Roman rule but the corruption of language that follows imperial domination. Slaughter and robbery go under the name of 'power' (we make much the same point about 'collateral damage'). And, in a now famous phrase, he says, 'They make a desert and call it peace.'

This is often treated, and quoted, as a barbarian denunciation of Roman rule. Of course, it is nothing of the sort. No real words of Calgacus or of any British 'barbarians' have survived. As with many imperial powers, the most acute critiques often came from within the Roman system, not from outside it. This is an analysis by Tacitus himself, a leading member of the Roman élite, observing the consequences of Roman expansion and daring to put himself into the place of the conquered.

As such, it makes an even more appropriate message for us. Whatever forms our 'deserts' take – whether it is the poppy fields of Afghanistan, or the ruins that will be left of Beirut, when Israel and Hezbollah (and our own culpable inactivity) have finished – we are still making them and calling them 'peace'.

The knife and fork test?

28 July 2006

There has been disappointing news about university entrants. The number of kids from state schools going to university has fallen. So has the number from the poorest families going to what are called 'leading universities'. So too (though no one seems quite so bothered about this one) has the number of boys.

News like this tends to provoke another round in the favourite national sport of Oxbridge bashing. The general line is that we sit round after dinner, quaffing our claret and plotting to let in thick privately educated toffs, and keep out the brightest and best from ordinary schools. Just occasionally this is backed up by a *cause célèbre*: an unlucky applicant with 15 A stars at GCSE and a raft of perfect A levels who was rejected, in favour (so the implication is) of a less qualified bloke who knew how to hold his knife and fork.

Everyone (apart from us) likes this kind of stuff. Tabloids push the hard luck story. The broadsheets play to the anxieties of a middle-class readership wondering if their children or grandchildren are going to make it. And for the Labour front bench, deploring the wickedness of élitist academics is a cheap way of reassuring the back bench rebels that they still have some kind of concern for social justice.

Of course, it's not like that at all. One problem with the *causes célèbres* is that rules of confidentiality stop us from telling our side of the story. The unsuccessful candidate's head teacher or parents can leak all they like about the unfortunate line of questioning ('You mean you've never been to the United States?') or the general bad treatment ('The interviewer was two hours late and then turned up in a dinner jacket').

We, by contrast, have to resort to general platitudes about the intensity of the competition and our 1000s of excellent applications with equally stellar paper qualifications. Sometimes that is the only explanation for rejection. But sometimes, I can assure you, there are other reasons why the apparently brilliant Miss X didn't get a place. And on those we must keep quiet.

But the more general point is that it is absolutely preposterous to imagine that people like me would choose to teach the stupid rich in preference to the bright poor. Of course, we make mistakes occasionally or we say things in interviews (usually quite inadvertently) that irritate or even upset a candidate. But for as long as I have been doing Cambridge interviews (over 20 years now) we have been pursuing intellectual potential, not social and cultural advantage.

The trouble is that the pursuit of potential is an inexact science. Let me give you an (entirely imaginary) example. On the one hand: Candidate A – a girl living with an unemployed grandmother in bed and breakfast accommodation, and attending a school from which only 5% of the pupils proceed to higher education, who has got 4 As at A level. On the other hand: Candidate B – a boy from an extremely expensive public school, whose Mum and Dad met at Cambridge before proceeding to lucrative legal careers, who also has 4 As. It is obvious that it has taken a lot more for Candidate A to get to this point than Candidate B and her potential may well be greater (and I'm as sure as I could be that she would get a place). But that does not mean that Candidate B does not deserve a place, too – and you couldn't rule out the possibility that he was actually cleverer. After all, geniuses come from posh homes as well as poor ones.

So we do our best. We get trained how to interview more fairly (no knife and fork tests or class-specific questioning). We visit schools to encourage the best to apply (and not to be put off by what they read in the paper). And we get all the data that we can. Despite some recent fuss about such an initiative at Oxford, for years we have been given 'adjusted A level scores' (which take account of their school's overall performance) for all our candidates. But frankly we are not helped by the fact that school references are now open to the applicant, so we get a lot less straight talking from head teachers than we used to.

The bottom line is that it is politically naïve (as well as unfair) for a government to underfund the state education system and to take little effective action on social justice, and then to blame 'leading universities' for not righting the wrongs they have perpetuated.

Keeping sex out of scholarship

1 August 2006

Sometimes I feel that people read what I write in a surprisingly perverse way. To put that more kindly, there is an odd mismatch in journalism (even the most cerebral literary kind of journalism) between the attention given to the writing and the attention given to the reading. I slave for hours trying to capture exactly the right nuance – then someone takes the *TLS* on the train or to the loo, gives it five minutes and goes away with a very odd impression of what I was trying to say.

Not that I blame the reader. After all, I probably give much the same 5-minute treatment to what other people write. And you might argue that it is the writer's job to make their point clear to all-comers. All the same, when someone completely misrepresents you, it is peculiarly irritating.

Last week, the *Independent* newspaper published a 'question and answer' article with the excellent Mary Warnock. One question was: 'Professor Mary Beard has suggested that Eduard Fraenkel's status as a classical scholar is diminished by his inappropriate conduct towards women in his Oxford classes … As a former student of Fraenkel's, do you agree?'

Warnock's reply: 'I think, alas, Professor Beard is talking nonsense.'

I would have been tempted to agree with Warnock myself, if that had been even remotely what I wrote.

What the questioner (whom I shall not name and shame) was referring to was a review I wrote in the *TLS* of a new *Dictionary of British Classicists*. In this I pointed out that it was very odd that the entry on Fraenkel (Professor of Latin in Oxford from 1935–53) made no mention of his notorious 'wandering hand' – clearly documented by (*inter alias*) Warnock herself in her autobiography.

I did not for a minute suggest that this diminished his status as a classicist. Classical scholars come equipped with all manner of sexual virtues and vices. And, by and large (there are, of course, some limitations), sex can be separated from scholarship. In fact I stuck my neck out to say that most women over their mid-40s (e.g. me) were likely to feel ambivalent about Fraenkel's behaviour. One can't help deploring the abuse of male power. But one also – honestly – can't help feeling a bit nostalgic for that, now outlawed, erotic dimension to (adult) pedagogy.

What I objected to was the bowdlerisation of the biographical tradition. When it is relatively widely known how Fraenkel spent his evenings with his female students, why does that have to be blotted out from the authorised version of his life? Why bother with the pretence that he was devoted solely to his wife? Or why not, at least, be prepared to see that devotion as part of a more complicated set of relationships? Don't we need to remember our intellectual giants warts and all?

That is not the same thing at all as questioning his scholarly status.

It could, of course, be worse. The status of Fraenkel is a decidedly minority interest. But a few years ago I wrote what I hoped was a similarly nuanced piece on reactions to 9/11. And ever after I've been that foolish/callous/dangerous don who thought that 'the United States had it coming'. Being traduced on Fraenkel isn't quite so bad.

But maybe I should have learnt my lesson.

Comments

I recall a heated University of London debate as to whether Blunt
should be stripped of his Emeritus title after the revelations about
his spying career. Only if it were proved that he had falsified data in
his catalogue *raisonné* of Poussin was the most rational response.

DEIRDRE

I was fortunate enough to be a pupil of Colin Macleod, who
studied under Fraenkel. On one occasion Colin confided: 'The
problem is, John, that some fine scholars discover too late that
what they are really interested in is golf, women or whatever'.
Fraenkel, along with others who shall remain nameless, fell into
the second group.

   In passing, I should mention that Colin was in a different class
from Fraenkel, who, like most Teutons, was encyclopaedic rather
than insightful. Colin's premature demise through suicide was one
of the greatest losses suffered by classical studies in Britain, and
indeed the world.

JOHN

Congratulations for being honest and understanding the powerful
link between learning and eroticism. I, a vehemently non-gay
male, once spent a whole night drinking with a notorious but
brilliant Cambridge don who tried to grope me; but the knowledge
and information I gained was immensely useful and could not
have been provided publicly (it concerned spying in a foreign
country). I knew what I was doing – although friends of mine were
shocked at breakfast in the morning to see me bleary-eyed with
him at the high table – and had no regrets.

EDWARD

In the harem

11 August 2006

I have never been to Istanbul before. So on my first visit, after some serious work on the antiquities, I made straight for the Topkapi Palace – HQ of the Ottoman rulers and the tourist high-spot of the city.

It was a nicely multicultural kind of tourism. Grubby backpackers in shorts rubbed shoulders with parties of headscarved (and gratifyingly badly behaved) Muslim school girls. Elderly guidebook-readers shared benches with elderly Muslim pilgrims – there to see the numerous relics of Mohammed himself that the Sultans had acquired.

I left the relics till last. And once I'd paid the money and passed the security check (liquids, thank heavens, were still allowed), I made straight for the harem.

You have to pay extra to visit the harem and technically speaking you can only go round with a guide (parties leave every half hour). But despite fierce notices about not getting separated from your group, none of the guards seemed too much bothered if you hired an individual 'audio guide' and wandered pretty much at will.

It's an extraordinary place, wonderfully decorated, with some of the best views in the whole palace – and its intricate social and sexual hierarchies, and mechanisms of surveillance, are built into the architecture. It was hard to work out exactly how everything fitted together (that was presumably part of the Sultan's point). But the basic principles were clear enough.

The favourite women had better accommodation and were closer to the Sultan than the less favourite; the eunuch guards could watch everyone coming and going, with the help, if necessary, of some very big mirrors.

It is the politics of the place that poses more problems. The old orientalist image of decadent and luxurious sexuality seems completely out of fashion (except on the postcards and Turkish Delight tins on sale outside the palace). My guidebook had replaced this with an image of sheer terror. The harem, it stressed, was 'a cut-throat environment ... the women manouevred, plotted, poisoned and knifed their way up the harem hierarchy'. And if the jealousies of the other women weren't enough, there was the murderous whim of the Sultan and his eunuchs. 'Some of them got their kicks stuffing girls in sacks, loading them into a boat and dumping them overboard in the Bosporus.' Two sultans apparently disposed of their whole harems that way.

So it came as a bit of a shock to find that the audio guide took a very different line. According to that commentator, the harem was a rather cultured kind of place. It was one of the few contexts in which a woman could learn the liberal arts – and from time to time the soundtrack played music that, we were assured, was actually written by a harem resident. Many of the girls apparently went on to make happy marriages with members of the Sultan's court. ('A bit like an Oxbridge woman's college', I kept thinking it was going to say – but it didn't.)

There is not much point trying to get to the bottom of this. For it's actually a classic example of how difficult we find it, from the outside, to understand what actually goes on inside all-woman institutions. In fact, it reminded me of all those dilemmas classicists face in working out how to make sense of the Greek poetess Sappho and her community of girls. Should we see her as a school mistress with a crush on her favourite pupils? Or was she more like a brothel-keeper? Or leader of a louche lesbian coven?

Who knows?

In the news in Pompeii

18 August 2006

I am still reeling from the reaction to my 'Keeping Sex out of Scholarship' blog. More than a year ago, I reviewed a book in the *TLS* (a *Dictionary of British Classicists*), in which I pointed out how the reliable stories of what is euphemistically known as the 'wandering hand' of Eduard Fraenkel, a Professor of Latin at Oxford, had been ignored. I wrote that I had an ambivalent reaction to what Fraenkel was supposed to have done: on the one hand, sisterly outrage at the abuse of male power; on the other, a wistful nostalgia (shared, I can assure you, by many of my age) for an earlier era of pedagogy, an age perhaps of greater innocence. What was the reaction? I received just a handful of letters from outraged pupils of Fraenkel, denouncing me for sullying the memory of their teacher.

A couple of weeks ago, I return to the issue briefly in a blog. This gets suddenly picked up by the media, from the *Mail* to the BBC. This time I am denounced for exactly the opposite crime. Now I am supposed to be the out-of-touch Cambridge don who 'hankers after' an age when professors slept with students. Not what I said, and not true.

Let me say again (I've found myself saying this often over the last couple of days), I do not condone sexual harassment or 'hanker after' a return to the old world. 'Wistful nostalgia' is a very different reaction – which doesn't involve trying to put the clock back. We can, after all, have wistful nostalgia for the nicotine culture of half a century ago, and the swirls of smoke around Bogart's head in *Casablanca*, without deciding to go out and buy a packet of Marlboro – and without being unaware that, if he went on like that, Rick would die a very unpleasant death from lung cancer.

By far the best encapsulation of the ambivalence I was trying to express is to be found in Mary Warnock's memoirs. Warnock was one of Fraenkel's 'girls' and she very nicely gets across both the sense that she had benefited from the high-octane pedagogy that he offered some of his favourites, and the sense that some students were terribly damaged by it.

For me, the whole reaction to what I wrote feels even odder because I am not even in the country. I am at Pompeii, getting some work in for the next book I should be getting on with. Yesterday, as I was exploring the site with the husband and an Italian colleague, the mobile phone kept going and re-going (the reception is a bit wobbly at Pompeii) – wanting quotes or more articles. What I decided not to say is that I was actually in the middle of an exploration of Pompeian so-called 'brothels', wondering what the criteria should be for identifying them. That would have been throwing too much of a delicacy to the wolves.

So what have I learned from all this? Well, first, be very careful what you say in the silly season of August. But, on the other hand, the reaction – silly and inaccurate as much of it is – shows that this a difficult subject that people do want to discuss. I would also advise friends and colleagues not to give an interview to the *Today* programme on a mobile phone from the back of a bar in Pompeii station. It's hard to get the point across!

Comments

The link between *eros* and pedagogy is well-established and made explicit by, among others, Plato – perhaps a clearer thinker than most journalists. What's alarming is that we have even come to suspect the coupling of, not *eros*, but *philia* with teaching. Shall we return to the days when teaching was in the hands of avowed celibates (and we know where THAT led)? Maybe so, in these curious times when we are scared of everything, just like a bunch of big babies.

But a couple of personal observations. My old headmaster once said to me that 90% of schoolmasters were paedophiles at heart – who else would want to spend his working life among adolescent males except one who genuinely loved them? The other 10%, of course, were pederasts, and they were the ones to keep an eye on. A distinction we have lost.

And, at the university level, I am proud to say that I was inducted into the pleasures of the bed by one of my supervisors, some 10 years older than I. It was an unalloyed joy – I hope, for both of us – and it stimulated not only my erotic sensibilities but also my interest in the subject she taught: two great gifts which have given me delight to this day. I will be grateful to her for ever, and my gratitude is only increased by the certainty that the withershins of anxious, unthinking PC will never know anything like it.

MICHAEL BYWATER

Fiddling while Rome burned

19 September 2006

Professional classicists have a habit of pouring cold water on popular facts about the ancient world. Take something that everyone thinks they know about Greece and Rome, and the finger-wagging scholar loves nothing better than saying it's wrong.

Well, for a change, the good news is that Nero did fiddle while Rome burned. It just depends what you mean by fiddle.

Most people, I fear, take 'fiddling' in the wrong sense.

This struck me when I was reading the previews in the weekend papers of the new BBC series of Roman drama-docs I've been involved with. The first episode features Nero (don't ask me to explain here and now, but the episodes don't move in chronological order: the 'earliest' programme, featuring Tiberius Gracchus, is actually episode three).

With good historical credentials, Nero is shown being an energetic and responsible emperor in the aftermath of the Great Fire of Rome in 64 AD. He provides emergency housing for the victims and sets about rebuilding the city in a way that wouldn't make it such a tinderbox in the future. This idea obviously appealed to the TV critics – more than one of whom wrote something along the lines of, 'So Nero did not fiddle while Rome burned. Rather he returned to his capital to help his people…' In fact, the same thought appeared so often that I began to suspect, correctly as it turned out, that they had lifted it straight from the BBC's own publicity material.

Hang on, thought the smirking don. These guys obviously think that Nero has wrongly been accused of 'fiddling' in the sense of 'footling around'. In fact, Nero's 'fiddling' was a wholly musical gesture. What the phrase refers to is his playing, if not the violin (= fiddle), then its nearest ancient equivalent, the lyre.

For, before he got into his emergency response mode, according to the historian Dio, he went up on the roof of the palace, put on his lyre-playing outfit and sang a song on an all too apt subject – the 'Fall of Troy'. Suetonius in his biography of Nero has a similar story of the singing (though minus the lyre). Nero's crime was not 'footling around'. It was that his first instinct in the face of crisis was to take refuge in the arts and high culture.

Whether we will ever now rescue what I think of as the 'real meaning' of this phrase is doubtful. In fact, it may be a better idea to celebrate the shift of meaning rather than pedantically lament it. It certainly makes it more easily applicable. When George W. Bush was widely accused of 'fiddling while Rome burned' as New Orleans drowned, I don't think his detractors had in mind a misplaced devotion to high culture.

What makes a good review?

29 September 2006

Reviews don't make a blind bit of difference to how a book sells. That, at least, is the popular wisdom among publishers. That means Jeffrey Archer's latest 'novel' can get rubbished by the critics and still make millions (the vast publicity budget presumably helps). Or, the other way round, there are thousand and thousands of marvellous books, greeted rapturously by reviewers, that have failed even to pay back their meagre advance. A nice review warms the heart of the author but it doesn't have much impact on the cash registers.

True. But it does rather underestimate the point of the whole reviewing business. Of course, working on the *TLS*, I'm biased – but I am committed to the idea that reviews have an important part to play in (for want of a better word) literary culture. Not only as a guide to the quality of what authors and publishers turn out, but also in their own right – as comment, criticism, insight, and a good read.

So how do I choose reviewers for the Classics books when I'm at the *TLS*? In a way it's a bit like a dating agency.

That is to say, the art of getting a good review (and by 'good' I don't mean 'favourable') is marrying up the right reviewer with the right book, even if at first sight they make an unlikely couple. I have three basic rules of thumb.

1 Never send a book to someone if you already know what they are going to say. Despite what people often think about the ethics of the reviewing trade, there really isn't

much interest, for me at least, in fixing up a review that merely hands someone a free platform for back-scratching or denunciation. Of course, sometimes you get it wrong … you publish a withering critique of someone's life's work, then a few months later a friend explains that the reviewer and reviewee had actually had a grudge match going on since the playground. But I can put my hand on heart and say that I've never knowingly done that. And I make it my business to keep abreast of people's quarrels!

2   Step outside the box. At first, you might think that a new book on (say) Ammianus Marcellinus, written by one of the two living experts on this (frankly not much read) late Roman historian, is best reviewed by the other one. In fact, he or she might be the worst of choices. For a start there's the last problem to bear in mind: the chances are that these guys have either long been riven in dispute over their unlikely favourite author, or are else best buddies. But, anyway, the acutest reviewer is often someone who works in a related but slightly different area, or someone who's long been a secret fan of Ammianus (you have to keep your ear to the ground in this trade) but has never actually written on him. That way you get the insider's and the outsider's perspective. Insider's: because you do want to learn from someone who knows whether this book basically passes muster. Outsider's: because you want someone who can represent the potential reader and can ask whether there's something interesting for us in all this.

3   Remember that it all takes time. Time from reviewers, to do a careful, interesting and well-written job. My heart sinks if I ever hear someone boasting how they knocked off a quick *TLS* review before breakfast. (I've been known to point out, waspishly, that it probably would have been a better review if

they had taken longer.) But also time from the commissioning editor. You need to explore beyond the front cover and the first few pages of the book you're sending out. If you want to arrange that delicate marriage with a reviewer, you really do have to have an idea what the book is saying (not what the blurb says it says). Put simply, a good review editor takes time to get to know their product on the inside.

A pity, after all this care and attention, that reviews don't have more impact on sales.

Freshers' week

2 October 2006

Tuesday is the beginning of the Cambridge academic year – and thousands of new students have turned up. Going through the elaborate welcoming routine, I find it impossible not to remember what it felt like more than 30 years ago when I was in their place.

For a start it was much less elaborate. Nowadays the kids go through almost a solid week of induction, so intensive that I can't imagine much of it goes in. There are briefings on Health and Safety, tours of the various libraries, computer training sessions, meetings with student reps of the Faculty, JCR tea parties and 'bops', plagiarism avoidance classes (well, almost) … and that is before they have been to meet any of their teachers and lecturers.

I remember it all being much more down to earth. A big college 'feast' with a pep talk from the Principal, a brief meeting with our Tutor and Director of Studies – and off we went, in at the deep end (and amazingly we did soon manage to fathom how the University Library worked).

Apart from the predictable anxieties and indiscretions of the first few days (which I do not intend to share!), I now remember only two things of those first encounters with the College Fellows.

The first was telling the Principal, mingling after her pep talk, that I did not intend to eat 'in hall' while I was at Newnham, but to make *coq au vin* (it was the 70s) in the student kitchens. I must have delivered this with unnecessary emotional force, since 30 years on she remembers our conversation too. The second was the meeting with my excellent, but appropriately terrifying, Director of Studies, who reminded us very firmly that we were at Cambridge at the expense of the tax-payer – and that tax-payers would expect us to work just as hard as they did: 40 hours a week, 48 weeks a year.

If someone had said to me then that just a few decades later I myself would be standing up in front of a new group of undergraduates, I would never have believed it – and frankly even now it's a bit hard to take in. What do you say? In my case, what am I going to say to the assembled first year classicists in the university – more than 80 of them – on Wednesday?

Well, sadly, you can't use the tax-payer line anymore. They'd probably lynch you. Most of these students, after all, are taking on a whacking debt for the privilege of a university education.

Most likely I shall concentrate, like last year, on the different kind of skills they will need at university from at school. Whatever the merits and demerits of the modern sixth-form curriculum, it certainly doesn't teach independent learning. When they arrive, they are used to a 'target' approach to education (if you make the following four points and show that you can recognise a subjunctive you will get an A). They also tend to imagine that the only time they are actually learning something is when someone is standing up in front of them, teaching them.

I shall try to convince them (with only a modicum of success, to judge by past performance) that intellectual endeavour goes beyond targets – and that the time when they really learn the most is probably not in the classroom but when they are by themselves, reading hard in the library.

The point I want them to grasp is that one of the aims of the devoted, skilled, inspirational and expensive teaching we offer is to give them the confidence to be able to explore the world of learning on their own.

Comments

You could try telling your students they are extremely lucky. I took my undergraduate degree with the Open University, and am taking my MA with the same organisation. We didn't have the huge asset of a university library on site, and really had to self motivate from day one. I am lucky to be situated reasonably close to a Classics library I can access, but my borrowing rights are not as generous as the 'on site' students. Our tutors are brilliant, but remote. And a substantial majority of us are holding down full time jobs while studying. I would give a great deal to be one of your students at Cambridge.

JACKIE

Veils, turbans and 'rivers of blood'

9 October 2006

Controversy about how other cultures and religions dress is centuries old – stretching at least as far back as ancient Roman anxieties about the flamboyantly coloured costume of the eastern priests of the goddess Cybele (also known as 'the Great Mother'). It's odd that most of those who have recently huffed and puffed on either side of the Jack Straw 'veil debate' seem to have forgotten the almost equally fierce arguments in the 1960s about a quite different article of religious clothing: Sikh turbans.

When I was a child growing up in the West Midlands, one of the big issues of multiculturalism (though we didn't yet call it that) was whether local Sikh bus drivers and conductors should be allowed to work with long beards and their traditional headdress. It provoked national debate and banner headlines no less doomladen than what we have seen and heard. Panic intensified after one Wolverhampton Sikh threatened to burn himself to death unless the prohibition was relaxed. There were rumoured to be many more prepared to follow his suicidal example.

Opinions were, of course, divided. Many Sikhs felt that their religion was being insulted by a prohibition on turbans. Others were uneasy about the hard line stance, worrying about the 'worsening of community harmony' that it might cause. But the problem was resolved when in 1969 the Wolverhampton Transport Authority gave in to the pressure. I cannot now remember what had caused their opposition in the first place. But, apart from the old-fashioned assumption that men on the buses would not be the same without peaked caps, I imagine it came down to some version of (in Straw's words) 'separation' and 'difference'.

Forty years on, Sikhs are still threatened by the endemic racism that even now affects the lives of anyone in this country who is not 'safely' white. And, since 9/11, there has been some unease in the New York transport department about traditional Sikh dress. But no one in Britain, apart from the lunatic fringe of the BNP, would surely think anything odd about a bus driver wearing a turban (and most of us would be only too delighted to have conductors back, whatever they were wearing).

It is hard at the distance of almost 40 years to recollect the intensity of feeling generated by this particular controversy. But it lay directly behind Enoch Powell's infamous 'Rivers of Blood' speech, delivered in Birmingham in 1968. Towards the end of this, he quoted the words of the then Labour MP and government minister John Stonehouse, decrying the stance of the local Sikhs and their campaign for the right to wear the turban.

'The Sikh communities' campaign,' said Stonehouse, in tones no better than Powell's, 'to maintain customs inappropriate in Britain is much to be regretted. Working in Britain, particularly in the public services, they should be prepared to accept the terms and conditions of their employment. To claim special communal rights (or should one say rites?) leads to a dangerous fragmentation within society. This communalism is a canker: whether practised by one colour or another it is to be strongly condemned.'

This was no straightforward party political issue.

Looking back at the full text of Powell's speech, you will find it springs a number of surprises. Not least, Powell never used the phrase 'rivers of blood'. He actually quoted a line from the sixth book of Virgil's *Aeneid*: 'I see the river Tiber foaming with much blood' ('*Et Thybrim multo spumantem sanguine cerno*', line 86). These are the words of the prophetic Sibyl, uttered to Aeneas, the refugee from Troy and ancestor of the Romans, on his way to re-establish his ancestral line on Italian soil.

Uncharacteristically, Powell seems to have overlooked the way the quotation might contradict his own arguments. True, the Sibyl was referring to the bloodshed that would result from Aeneas' attempt to found his new city in Latin territory, integrating his own line into that of the native population. But that bloodshed would lead to a strong and proudly mixed community of Trojans and Latins. And Aeneas' Rome in due course would become the most successful multicultural society of the ancient world – granting full citizenship to the inhabitants of its imperial territories, and eventually seeing Spaniards, Africans and others on the Roman imperial throne.

Sikh turbans or not, Powell should have thought a bit harder about the implications of his clever classical allusion.

Comments

An analogy from a different epoch offers other morals: When the king of Hungary was doing badly in the then war on terror (aka crusade against the Ottomans) in 1463, he tried to divert attention by accusing his neighbour the prince of Wallachia of cruelty. The famous bit is that this guy (known to posterity as Vlad

the Impaler) impaled his victims on stakes; a lesser known piece
of spin against him was that when Italian ambassadors came
to see him they took off their hats but not their turbans – yes,
Italians wore turbans back then – and that Vlad, angered at this
discourtesy, allegedly nailed them down to their wearers' heads.
Back then, intolerant response to strange customs was something
shameful to accuse your rival of doing, not something to be
boasting about to the press.

SW FOSKA

Where is your spleen?

13 October 2006

This week I started my lectures on Ancient History to first year students. Following a tradition invented by one of my colleagues 20 years ago, I kicked off the very first lecture by handing round a skeletal map of the Mediterranean – and asked them to mark several key places (including Athens, Sparta, Troy, Crete, Rome and Pompeii). The results are collected in for scrutiny, but entirely anonymously. No names are required.

The idea is to demonstrate to the freshers that they really do need to get an atlas out before they start sounding off about the Peloponnesian War, or whatever. The accuracy this year was no better or worse than usual. Most of my 100 or so clever first years could place Rome and Pompeii, but Sparta wandered dangerously (from time to time popping up in modern Turkey) while Alexandria was a mystery to many, and one at least appeared not to know that Crete was an island. Are they pulling my leg? I wondered ...

Over the decades this little exercise has given the new students a wonderful feeling of shared ignorance. The dons, on the other hand, have enjoyed shaking their heads at the very idea that a student with straight (classical) As at A level still doesn't know where Sparta is.

We don't of course blame the students – but the government or the National Curriculum. Our students are, we believe, the *crème de la crème*. The trouble is that they have been let down by the 'system' before they came to us. (Better not to ask if we, aged just 18, could have marked Alexandria on a map … but that's another story.)

For centuries, dons have combined a loving over-commitment to their students with a rhetoric that deplores the ignorance of those they are teaching. The 'Can-you-believe that-they-have-never-heard-of-Pericles?' line is one of the most primitive and powerful of all donnish bonding rituals.

This struck me very strongly this week when I rushed from that first year lecture to steal an hour of work in the University Library. I was there to look up some of the pamphlets of the 1860s written at the height of Victorian debates about what should or should not be taught in schools and universities. If anyone now thinks that education is over-politicised, they should try the nineteenth century. Those Victorian gurus debated even more furiously than our own the rights and wrongs of the curriculum. And they were just as ready to blame the 'government'.

I found myself reading a tract by Robert Lowe (Chancellor of the Exchequer immediately before Gladstone), denouncing the tyranny of Latin and Greek over the school syllabus. He lingered, like me, to think of what the *crème de la crème* did not know – because, in his view, they had been kept to a narrow classical path.

'I will now give you a catalogue of things which a highly educated man may be in total ignorance of,' he wrote. 'He probably will know nothing of the anatomy of his own body. He will have not the slightest idea of the difference between the arteries and the veins, and he may not know whether the spleen is placed on the right or the left side of his spine. He may have no knowledge of the simplest truths of physics and would not be able to explain the barometer or thermometer.'

Sounds familiar? My first thought was to get a new questionnaire up for next week to see how my students did on these central issues of basic science. Until I realised that I would be hard pressed myself to say on which side of my spine my spleen lay. In fact it was probably the likes of me (though you would have to change the gender) that Lowe had in mind.

As these Victorians saw, there is an issue here not just about what facts people should know, but about what education is for, and who is responsible for it. Our generation tends to think that we are the first to have wondered about this. Far from it.

A captive audience

23 October 2006

Classics offers more interesting speaking opportunities than you might imagine. In addition to the talks at schools, colleges, breakfast clubs, museums and the like, I occasionally get a more surprising gig. Some recent favourites have been pre-performance talks at the Coliseum (engaging the audience with the myth of, say, Semele before they see what Handel did with it) and a guest appearance at the wonderful 'Treasury Women's Group' (though that was more in the guise of female academic than strictly classicist).

But most memorable of all have been the couple of occasions I have gone to lecture to the inmates at a high-security prison. It's an extraordinarily electric kind of teaching. Partly because it's one of the few (relatively) free opportunities that they have for face to face interchange with the outside world, they give it far more attention than your average audience – half of whom are worrying if they'll make the bus/ have time to get to the supermarket/meet their girlfriend when you've finished speaking. No chance of that for these guys.

A captive audience, as colleagues couldn't resist – a bit predictably – joking.

On one of these occasions I talked to them about Roman gladiators and the blood and guts of the Roman arena. It wasn't long before some bright spark observed that the horrors I was describing would have been their own fate, as convicted criminals, had they lived in the ancient world. True. But what really surprised them was the fact that the Romans did not, by and large, use detention as a punishment. Roman prisons were for holding people before trial or before execution. In fact, much the same was true in Europe until the eighteenth century, when punishment-by-detention became the norm.

I resisted the temptation to say to them what I really thought – that in two thousand years' time our contemporary obsession with incarceration will seem as weird to future historians as the gladiatorial games now seem to us. Sure, they will observe, some criminals presented a real danger to the rest of the population. But what on earth drove a sophisticated society to bang up even those who presented no physical danger at all, in an over-crowded community of other criminals – out of which some 75% emerged (surprise, surprise) to commit another crime within two years? How could they not have seen that it was a mechanism for the repetition (not prevention) of crime, and an extremely costly one at that? It takes considerably more than the average annual wage to keep a prisoner inside for a year.

This isn't primarily the fault of those who work in prisons. The people I have met staffing education departments are doing a heroic job in trying to give some of their charges a leg up, and out of crime. But they are terribly under-resourced, and the frequent moving of prisoners from one gaol to another makes any continuity of instruction really hard. In general, the prison service seems to be doing its best, as you sense if you look at the literature they issue for prisoners and others – even if the rhetoric occasionally misfires. (I thought that the phrase 'in-cell television is being gradually introduced as an earnable privilege, but it may not be available in your prison' sounded uncomfortably like one of those airline notices 'we apologise if your first choice of meal is not available …')

Things will only change when the public and the tabloid press have been convinced that incarceration is not the answer. And that will take a Home Secretary with more muscle and vision than any we have had for decades.

What did the Romans wear under their togas?

27 October 2006

If you teach at Oxford or Cambridge, you get used to the regular bursts of outrage about 'the Oxbridge interview'. I posted a few months back about the myth that we are all a load of upper-class twits who use the interview to pick students just like ourselves. Wrong on both counts.

Just recently a different variant was doing the rounds: the one about all those weird, donnish and – this is the subtext – UNFAIR questions we ask at the interviews. Just to make sure the poor squirming candidate never feels at ease. A whole list of them were reeled off in the press and even on the *Today* programme. 'What percentage of the world's water is contained in a cow?' (Veterinary Medicine, Cambridge). 'Are you cool? (Philosophy, Politics and Economics, Oxford). 'Why can't you light a candle in a spaceship? (Physics, Oxford). The *Evening Standard* even dredged up some celebs to have a go at answering them – not very well.

What did not get headlined was the fact that the survey that had brought all these questions to light had been commissioned, and then hyped, by a company which specialises in helping potential students prepare for their Oxbridge interview – for a fee. There's nothing like a bit of media panic to send frightened kids (and their over-anxious parents) rushing off with their cheque books to get some 'specialist' advice.

My thoughts on this will, I hope, be reassuring. More than that, they are free.

The first thing that any student going to an interview needs to remember is that we are wanting to let people in, not keep them out. Of course, it may not feel like that to the kid on the receiving end. And, of course, we have many more applicants than there are places. Not everyone can be successful. That said, we are trying at the interview to get each candidate to show themselves at their very best. We want to see how good they are, not how bad.

Sometimes this takes surprising forms, as with those odd questions. Everyone who conducts these interviews will tell you that over-preparation is as damaging to a candidate's chances as under-preparation. I have often sat and listened to some hopeful reeling off, unstoppably, a prepared speech on the perfection of the Virgilian hexameter or why the Spartans won the Peloponnesian War. Bowling them a googly ('So what do you think the Romans wore under their togas?') is sometimes the only way of throwing them a lifeline – of giving them the opportunity to show that they can think independently, not from the prepared script.

So if I was giving one piece of advice to those preparing for an interview in my subject? Much cheaper than being professionally 'groomed' – I would go out and buy (or borrow) a book about any aspect of the ancient world that interests you and one that is not a mainline part of your school syllabus, or takes you beyond it. Read it; know its title (you'd be surprised how many interviewees can only remember the colour of the dust jacket of their favourite reading matter); and be prepared to talk about it if you are asked – but no prepared speeches, remember.

Happily, this is not entirely inconsistent with another aspect of the interview survey that did not get so much media coverage. Apparently almost 40% of the philosophy candidates who had read Mill's *Utilitarianism* got a place ... as well as the impressive 75% of all candidates (for any subject, apparently) who regularly read the *Economist*.

By the way, I don't think I shall be interviewing this year. So please don't anyone go wasting their time trying to find out what Romans did wear under their togas. Anyway, sorely tempted as I have been, I have never actually asked the question. In fact, I don't think we know the answer. But if I were to ask it, the point of the question (apart from stopping the unstoppable prepared script) would be to see if the candidate could begin to think through the limits of our ignorance about antiquity, as well as imagine how you might go about filling in the gaps. It wouldn't be a 'trick' at all.

Comments

Wasn't it a *subligaculum*, which my old school pocket dictionary defines as a 'loin cloth'? Go on! Tell me I'm wrong!

DAVID KIRWAN

David – I couldn't say you were wrong. But, as always with such things, the translation 'loin cloth' gets away with murder. It sounds appropriately antique (we don't wear them now, after all) ... but what do we think it actually looked like? Do we ever hear about someone taking their *'sublig'* off ...? There's a challenge.

MARY

Cicero (if I translate him correctly) says that no actor would
appear on stage without his *subligaculum*.

DAVID KIRWAN

Cicero seems to imply that actors without a *subligaculum* would
be open to the mischance of accidental indecent exposure
and that is why they wear it. Perhaps this doesn't apply to fine
upstanding citizens like Cicero. Meanwhile, before someone else
does, let me mention the 'bikini pants' worn by the girls on the
Piazza Armerina mosaics.

BINGLEY

Surely, if you rule the known world with an iron fist, you can wear
whatever you damned well please underneath your toga.

BENJAMIN WARREN

Don't you see, the question of what is worn under the toga is
precisely what is unfair about the interview!

Having codified the actual line of inquiry ('What are the limits
of our knowledge about the antiquities and how can we overcome
them, to some extent?') in an off-puttingly flippant remark, you
leave it up to luck whether the candidate will dare to climb down
from their anxiety about the situation and engage with your very
insensitive tone at complete ease.

How many clever, creative, talented students would simply go,
'Oh Christ, that's one of those Cambridge Questions that you can't
have an answer to!' How many would be blasted off their stride?

For goodness' sake, the Finals aren't written in that kind
of paracryptic style, so why on earth should you so phrase the
questions given to students who are at a Sixth-Form level, who will

be thinking that they are arrived at one of life's most defining and important moments (regardless if this is true)?

The ridiculous distinction between your paragraph-length explanation and your glib example cry out for the simple response: 'Just ask them the bloody question you had in mind!'

UTTERLY DISGUSTED

The sign of the cross

6 November 2006

I couldn't quite believe my ears when I was listening to the Archbishop of Canterbury head to head with John Humphrys on his new radio programme.

For those of you who don't follow the highlights of BBC Radio 4, Humphrys – the rottweiler of the *Today* programme and a religious sceptic – has a new series in which he interviews faith leaders to see if they can provide some convincing reasons to believe. Part of the appeal of this is to see whether he gives these venerable gentlemen the kind of treatment he usually metes out to some hapless junior minister. 'Let me be quite clear. You're claiming that God does not have a beard.'

First up was Rowan Williams. He's a very clever man, who held a lectureship in Cambridge and a Chair in Oxford before moving on to higher things. The interview in fact had more of the feeling of a Cambridge supervision than a *Today* programme grilling. But Williams got into severe difficulties at various points.

After coming close to denying that serious violence had ever been committed in the name of Christianity, he eventually admitted the Crusades had been 'a bad episode' – which is a classic example of being economical with the truth. And he really didn't seem to have the bottle to tell Humphrys, who was pressing him on this issue, that unless he mended his religious ways he was liable – according to the rule book – to end up in a rather fiery place after death.

But this isn't why I was really interested, it was because of what Williams had to say about the relations between pagans and Christians in the Roman empire – a subject which is close to my own academic patch.

It was in the context of whether Christians have a track record of forcing their views on others, either now or then. Williams seemed to feel on safer ground with the early church than with the modern world. To quote him, as I remember (and helped out by the script on the BBC website):

> It's what happened at the very beginning of the church's life. The church didn't simply blaze out into the Greco-Roman world saying, 'Here's the truth. You must believe it.' They said, 'Look – this is what *you* say, and that's very interesting as it echoes with what *we* say; and, if we talk this through, you might find that what you're saying has a much fuller expression in what we're saying.

If this is Williams's view of relations between Christians and pagans (or, should we less prejudicially say 'polytheists'?), then he's been reading a different selection of early Christians texts from me. There may be some parts of high-minded Christian philosophy that see things in these terms. And St Augustine certainly had a soft spot for classical Roman learning (especially Cicero). But most of the surviving tracts purvey a mixture of horrified outrage (at such ideas of animal sacrifice to the Roman emperor) and knockabout ridicule (of, for example, the goings-on of the various immoral gods and goddesses).

He must have read them – so has he simply forgotten the writings of that hard-line Christian ideologue Tertullian, who certainly had no truck with any part of traditional paganism? And has he forgotten the rather more appealing Minucius Felix, who tells a whole series of jokes about just how stupid is the idea of a multitude of gods in human form? And what about the pagan reaction to all this? Even if it wasn't as continuous a persecution as we often imagine, some Christians really did end up with the lions.

The touchy-feely view of Greco-Roman ecumenism has, I am afraid, more to do with the generous, academic tolerance of the Archbishop himself than with anything thought or practised by the motley crew of fundamentalist early Christians and what some Romans saw as an ancient Jihad.

Comments

Always nice to catch a glimpse of an archbishop with his truth-pants round his ankles ... He's claiming authority for what he sees is desirable by asserting it was like that 'in the beginning'. A not unusual sleight of hand. If historiography were studied properly, as a branch of rhetoric, there'd be a word for it. Or maybe there is already?

SW FOSKA

Being in exile in America, I did not hear the Archbishop, but I must say that the sentence of Rowan Williams which you quote seems to me to sum up rather neatly the massive *Praeparatio Evangelica* of Eusebius, an author to whom he alludes rather frequently in his *Arius: Heresy and Tradition* (one of the few accounts of the Arian controversy that is both learned and readable). Both Eusebius and the quoted sentence of Dr Williams are concerned with what pagans *said*, not with what they *did*. Your own work, Professor Beard, has been concerned much more with what Romans did, and that Christians (pardonably?) found at best so irrational that they were prepared to be killed as the penalty for not taking part in it.

OLIVER NICHOLSON

The tragedy of George Bush

13 November 2006

Classicists have to take any opportunity they can get to put –
or keep – their subject on the map. So when a nice man from
the *Today* programme rang up to say that they wondered if
I would like to compare the fate of George Bush to a Greek
tragedy, I could hardly say no.

The idea was that in the very same week that Saddam
had been sentenced to death he had also (albeit indirectly)
delivered a humiliating blow to Bush in the mid-term
elections. It is indeed the kind of tragic reversal that Athenian
dramatists discussed, and I quickly agreed to do a 3 minute
radio essay.

But which tragedy was I going to choose for the closest
parallel to GW?

At times like this, my colleagues are truly wonderful. It
would be quite understandable if they were to say: 'If you want
to thrust yourself forward on to the nation's radios, that's fine
… but don't expect us to help you out.' But actually we are
all happy to lend a hand and knocking the question around
produced some good leads very quickly.

I had wondered about concentrating on Sophocles'
Oedipus. The idea would be that Oedipus killed his long-lost
father in an incident of ancient road rage – and it was that
action which later brought him down, when it was revealed
that he had inadvertently married his mother. But father-
killing seemed to bring in Bush senior rather awkwardly and
probably muddied the waters.

Sophocles' *Trachiniae* ('Women of Trachis') looked a neater
fit. The story here is that Heracles kills the centaur Nessos
(who has tried to rape his wife, Deianeira). As the centaur dies,
he gives Deianaira some of his blood, which he says will keep
her husband from loving anyone else. When Heracles is later
unfaithful, she uses the blood to kill him. The trouble with this
is that hardly anyone is remotely familiar with the Trachiniae
and getting it across in a 3 minute piece wasn't going to leave
much time for Bush.

So, talking it over during lunch in college, I settled on
Euripides' *Bacchae*. The reversal is there good and clear: King
Pentheus of Thebes sentences to death the god Dionysos (in
disguise as a 'Lydian stranger') who has infected the women
of the city with his weird Eastern religion and enticed them
out to roam wild in the mountains. But the stranger/Dionysos
breaks out of prison miraculously and encourages Pentheus to
go to the mountains to see for himself. There he is torn limb
from limb by a posse of women led by his mother.

True, Saddam is not a god in disguise. But there are some
other features of the *Bacchae* that resonate nicely with the
Bush problem: it is partly set up as a clash between West and
East; the older and wiser statesmen of Thebes advise Pentheus
to resist the use of force (preferring talks and a negotiated
settlement); and much of the debate hinges on the theme of
Pentheus' unwillingness even to try to understand cultural
norms other than his own.

It went out on Saturday morning when the nation
slumbered, just before 'Thought for the Day' (indeed my
husband, still in bed, thought it WAS 'Thought for the Day').
But I'd love to know if anyone can think of a better parallel.
Indeed, was mine plausible at all?

Comments

Generally can't hack these attempts to lend portentous epic aura to predictably crap public débâcles. Would prefer to gaze upon them calmly without festooning them with unbecoming pity or wonder. The present predicament reminds me more of something from *Tom & Jerry* than Euripides.

SW FOSKA

I'm surprised you didn't go for something around the Trojan War – *Agamemnon* (Clytemnestra as the avenging Democrats, perhaps) or *Women of Troy*.

PAUL STEEPLES

Surely Aeschylus' *Persae*? Overweening monarch of a vast empire sees his troops overwhelmed by a tin-pot (in his view) anarchic (in his view) republic which has incurred his wrath by interfering in the internal affairs of his empire and burning one of his cities (Sardis).

DAVID KIRWAN

Pissing on the pyramids

22 December 2006

If you venture deep inside the pyramids, as I did on my Egyptian 'holiday', you find that the inner chamber smells very strongly of piss. It's a predictable act of desecration, I guess. But it does tend to encourage a speedy visitor turnaround.

In general, though, the pyramids sprang lots of surprises. And they offered the possibility of pleasures (or transgressions) that would be decidedly off limits back home.

Let me say to begin with that, unlike so many 'Wonders of the World', they do not disappoint. They are absolutely vast and, at least if you view them from one direction, they give every impression of being isolated in the trackless desert.

Visitors are not encouraged to look the other way, where the huge silhouettes appear not against the background of the camel-dotted sands, but against the suburbs of Cairo – and, in particular, against the distinctive colours of the Kentucky Fried Chicken outlet (Pyramids branch). It doubles with Pizza Hut if you go upstairs.

But, smell apart, the best bit was climbing inside, right into the burial chamber of the Great Pyramid. This is what British Health and Safety regulations would long ago have put a stop to. The climb is steep, with just a handrail and ridged wooden planking to help you. It's fantastically hot, even in December. And for a good stretch of the way you have to crouch down and almost crawl along a low passage to reach the heart of the monument.

Heaven knows what would happen if you didn't make it. There wasn't a defibrillator, alarm, or any other of the paraphernalia of the nanny state in sight. It makes it all seem faintly ridiculous that some governmental Risk Assessment doesn't allow the average visitor even to touch the stones of Stonehenge (might they fall down?), but insist that we gawp from a safe but boring distance.

Not that the Egyptian Antiquities Service makes a visit to the pyramids any easier than one to Stonehenge. You have to buy a ticket to get into the main area, pass through the metal detector and by the tourist police with their guns (Egypt gives a very plausible impression of being a relatively cheery police state, 'for your protection, sir' as they say). It's only when you've climbed up to the entrance way on the pyramid itself that they tell you that you have to buy another ticket, from somewhere completely different, if you want to go inside. And it's only when you have got back one more time that they tell you that you can't take your camera inside. It would clearly be asking for it to leave your precious digital on the little shelf suggested (when we went, it was the resting place for just one 'throwaway' camera); so you have to climb down again to leave it in the car – or, as we did, disguise it in a make-up bag.

And all this has to be done while avoiding the pushiest touts (plus camels) anywhere in the world. Exactly what scams they were trying to pull off wasn't clear; but scams they certainly were. Our driver insisted, like an anxious parent of thoughtless adolescents, that we spoke to no one, that we didn't wander round the back of the monument (where presumably even worse scammers lay in wait) and that we didn't hire the first camel from the first Bedouin we saw.

Still, it was probably the most memorable sight I've ever seen. And December was the perfect time to visit. Apart from a handful of intrepid Europeans, most of the visitors were local school parties. The little girls sweated through the passages in their veils and headscarves. But (much to the annoyance of their teachers) found us rather more exotic and photogenic a sight than the antiquities.

Comments

The overpowering smell of urea/ammonia is caused more by bat droppings than by human piss, I think.

AJM

Sex on the Beach

My prize Christmas present this year was an extremely elegant cocktail shaker, plus all the trimmings. And I mean all: four Martini glasses with flashing stems (improbably acquired from Marks & Spencer); cocktail recipe book; bottle of Cointreau and bottle of tequila (who would keep tequila in the house if they were not making cocktails?); and, to complete the kit, 12 limes (ditto, as for the tequila).

After a day's stint in the library, honestly, I need a stiff drink. So this Christmas it's been good-bye gin and tonic or a delicate glass or two of white wine; and hello Blue Lagoon and Moscow Mule.

What I like about cocktails is their total artfulness. There is nothing remotely 'natural' about them. In fact, the whole point is to get as far from the appearance and the taste of the 'real' ingredients as you can. I mean, there is no purpose whatsoever to blue curaçao except to turn some other innocent spirit that glorious shade of luminescent blue. Of course, it adds to the alcohol content, but it didn't need to be blue to do that.

There is also something wonderfully democratising about cocktails. OK, some mixtures are more naff than others. Those who fancy a nice dry Manhattan might well turn their noses up at a Tijuana Taxi. And a bit of snobbery comes into the making of Martinis (though even the latest Bond movie pokes fun at the 'shaken or stirred?' obsession). But there's none of that pretentious wine mythology involved. You don't have to sniff them or discuss the year. You just drink them. If you like the taste, you have another; if not, you change the mixture.

The history of the cocktail is a bit of a mystery. It certainly doesn't go back beyond the nineteenth century – and there's a strong hint that disguising the taste of the foul home-brewed spirits under Prohibition had something to do with their popularity. It struck me, in the middle of my second Margarita the other evening, how much the ancient Romans (the rich ones, at any rate) would have enjoyed the art of the cocktail if only they had thought of it.

Romans were refreshingly uncultured when it came to alcohol. They mostly mixed their wine with water and/or honey, and they didn't much care about vintages (except when they fell on an important political anniversary). So far as I know, they hadn't invented spirits – for drinking, that is. With uncharacteristic innocence, the only use the ancients found for distillation was industrial cleaning.

But it's the colour of cocktails that would most have appealed to those (bad) emperors who put such efforts into dining. The emperor Domitian hosted a marvellous 'black dinner' in the 80s AD – with not just the food colour-coded, but the skin of the waiters, too. Even better were the excesses of my own particular favourite Elagabalus, emperor between 218 and 222 AD. He did all you could hope a bad emperor would do (he is even said to have had a surgical sex change). But one of his specialities was banqueting. Apart from the famous trick with the rose petals (they were sprinkled so profusely that they smothered the guests), he was said to be especially keen on the 'themed' dinner party. Every day of the summer he gave a banquet in a different colour, now a green one, the next an 'iridescent' one, then blue.

Just think what fun he could have had complementing all this with Blue Lagoons, or a glorious green St Patrick's Day – a daring concoction of crème de menthe, Chartreuse, whiskey and Angostura bitters.

(By the way, if you were drawn to read this blog by its title, I guess you will now realise that I was referring to the cocktail, Sex on the Beach: 1 oz. peach schnapps, ¾ oz. vodka, topped with cranberry and orange juice ...)

Exams are getting harder – shock

16 January 2007

Yesterday I was sent an intriguing present. It was the exam papers taken by a Newnham Classics student in 1901–1902. I'd seen these before, in their pristine, bound volumes in the University Library. But actually fingering the ones that come direct from the exam room, still marked with the blood, sweat and tears of the poor student (well, almost) makes a more powerful impression.

It's hard not to ask yourself the obvious question: are these degree exams really more difficult than what our students do, like the gloomy commentators claim?

Well, put aside any romantic nostalgia for the glory days of rigorous classical education at the turn of the nineteenth and twentieth centuries. The good news is that what our undergraduates face at the beginning of the twenty-first is actually rather more challenging.

True, these papers *look* a bit more formidable (something to do with the close set typeface, I think), and there was a gruelling run of two three-hour papers per day (our students take only one a day). And you certainly had to *know* a lot. But there isn't much evidence that a lot of *thinking* was required. Imagine the brightest and best classicists sitting down after three years at Cambridge to: 'Mention the chief works of Zeuxis, Timanthes, Nikias and Timomachos' (a question about ancient painting, for which you just need to know the relevant passage of the elder Pliny). Or 'Describe with a sketch-plan the Circus Maximus at Rome'.

My favourite is the one that asked for 'a short description, showing where possible its evolution in classical times' of the 'lock and key'.

Now maybe it's charming to think of generations of students mugging up the workings of the ancient equivalent of a Yale lock. But our kids have more thinking to do. The question from last year's paper 'What role did religion play in policing sexual practice?' would have floored most of the class of 1901–1902 for more than the obvious reason. So too the tricky: 'Did physical beauty have moral value in classical Greece?'

But, you might be wondering, what about the more specialist linguistic tests? It's one thing to deal with this modern style of 'think question', but surely the students of a hundred years ago were asked to undertake much more difficult exercises translating from Latin and Greek.

Again, I'm not so sure. There was certainly a lot of it in the old papers, and they must have had to work at a cracking pace. But the passages from ancient authors they were asked to translate are not so very different from now. In fact, something very close to one passage from Cicero in 1901–1902 was set just last year.

The funniest comparison, though, is between what those students were asked to translate into Latin and Greek, and what ours do. Turning English into classical prose and poetry was one of the mainstays of a Classics degree a hundred years ago. It no longer has that central position, but it's an option that many of our students still choose (particularly translation into prose – verse is rather more arcane).

The papers of 1901–1902 are full of passages from Bishop Berkeley and the like to be rendered in Latin; plus some choice extracts from Tennyson and Dryden to go into verse. Last year

our students had more fun. They had some Seamus Heaney
and David Bowie to turn into Greek and Latin poetry.

Of course, it's a dangerous business comparing exams
across the decades, especially when (in the case of 1901–1902)
we only have the questions and no idea what the answers
looked like. (Maybe those answers on the lock and key would
have surprised me.) But there's not much ammunition here
for those who think classical, or university, standards have
dramatically slipped.

Racism in Greece and Rome

22 January 2007

I didn't actually watch Jade Goody and friends attack Shilpa
Shetty. But it's been impossible to avoid the endless follow-up
wrangling about what was really going on. Was this appalling
racism? An episode in the class war? Brutal bullying? Or just
plain hatred of foreigners (which, though unpleasant enough,
is not necessarily racist)?

It all reminded me uncannily of the debates about whether
racism existed in the Greek and Roman world.

There is no doubt at all that they often treated outsiders
badly. The idea of the 'barbarian' (someone whose speech
is just an incomprehensible 'ba ba') is a well known Greek
invention. But the cultural identity of both societies was
even more pervasively based on what we would now see as
an unhealthy distrust of anyone different from themselves.
Xenophobia, in other words.

The list of unnatural things that foreigners were supposed
to get up to is a long one. It ranged from peculiar eating habits
(not just frogs legs or poppadoms, but at its worst cannibalism)
to strange régimes of hygiene (women standing up to piss was
a notable source of wonderment and/or disdain) and topsy-
turvy ideas of sex and gender (women in charge).

The Greeks painted a contemptuous picture of the Persians
as trousered, decadent softies who wore far too much perfume.
Then the Romans came along and, minus the trousers, said
much the same about the Greeks: a nice example of being
given a taste of your own medicine.

But, strikingly, it's usually claimed that neither Greeks nor Romans bothered very much about skin colour. This was a time 'before colour prejudice'.

It's certainly the case that there seems to have been no general idea of social, cultural or intellectual inferiority based on the colour of a person's skin. There was no homogeneous slave class, of a different race and colour from their masters. And, in fact, exactly what skin colours were represented, and in what numbers, in the multicultural population of the Roman empire is something of a puzzle. The second-century AD emperor Septimius Severus, who came from modern Libya, may not have been black (even though that is sometimes argued); but then he probably wasn't as white as some of his marble busts make him seem either.

Ancient stories too suggest a very different set of assumptions about blackness and whiteness. There is a marvellous episode which touches just this subject in the *Aethiopica* (*Ethiopian Story*), a novel by Heliodorus, a third-century AD Greek writer from Syria. Persinna, the black queen of Ethiopia, with a black husband, gave birth to a white daughter. How did she explain it? She had been looking at a picture of (white) Andromeda at the time of the girl's conception.

But is it all quite so simple? Probably not. There's a recent book by Ben Isaac, *The Invention of Racism in Classical Antiquity*, which claims to have identified if not racism, then at least 'proto-racism' in the ancient world. Isaac insists (as do most serious analysts) that racism goes beyond casual xenophobia. It is a deterministic ideology, which sees some groups as unalterably inferior, thanks to natural or inherited characteristics. In modern society, the key natural characteristic has been skin colour.

Not so in the ancient world. But Isaac thinks he can identify something similarly deterministic (and so racist) in other, quite different natural factors. For him, the ancients were not *colour*-prejudiced; instead they were *geographical* and *environmental* determinists. To over-simplify a bit, he charges the Greeks and Romans with being 'proto-racists' in the sense that they believed that the characteristics which certain races derived from their (inferior) environment and from the climate in which they lived – the rain and fog of northern Europe, for example – were fixed and irreversibly inferior.

I'm not sure I wholly buy this line. But if just some of the sophistication of these debates about the ancient world, and about what racism might be, had been in evidence in all the huffing and puffing about Jade Goody and her faults, more sense might have been spoken.

Comments

The Jade Goody business had absolutely nothing to do with racism however interpreted (unless one accepts the Norman Mailer idea – which I do – that class in Britain is merely a form of racism). Essentially it was a superb classic example of pure British bullying produced by a tragic sense of low physical, intellectual and class esteem (irrespective of personal riches) in the bullier. Indeed, this was so clear that the 'racism' outcry was essentially an attempt by an embarrassed nation to divert this painful social fact of British life into the safer limited world of race.

LORD TRUTH

Paganism without the blood

26 January 2007

One of the good things about working on ancient 'pagan' religion is that no one actually believes in it any more. ('Pagan' here is in inverted commas, of course, because it wasn't a term people ever used of themselves: it was a term of semi-abuse from the Christian camp, and probably meant something like 'hick' or 'hillbilly'.)

It's easy to debate paganism because you're not always looking over your shoulder at a community of contemporary believers. Whenever I try to teach the 'rise of Christianity' with a group of undergraduates – did economics underlie it? the institutional support of the emperor Constantine? – I'm always horribly aware that part of the group doesn't really think it's a question worth asking. For them the obvious reason that Christians won out against the pagans was that their religion was true. Simple as that.

In contrast, paganism is a teacher's joy. You can dissect it as fiercely as you like. You can even claim that Zeus, Aphrodite and co. did not actually exist, without fear of being arraigned on a charge of incitement to religious hatred.

Or so I thought. But last week a group of modern Athenians, dressed in ancient Greek costume (so they claimed), descended on the Temple of Olympian Zeus in Athens, prayed to Zeus to bring about world peace and held a ceremony to celebrate the marriage of Zeus and Hera. A few months before they had gained official recognition as a religious organisation from the Greek government.

At first sight not good news for me. But on closer inspection I needn't have worried.

It isn't entirely clear what this group ('Ellenais') believes; but it *is* clear that, whatever they say, it bears very little relationship to ancient Greek religion. You can tell that already from the rather charming prayer to Zeus to bring about world peace. From an ancient point of view, whatever myths are peddled about the 'Olympic Truce', there could hardly be a less likely divine candidate for putting a stop to war in the world.

So far as I can tell, they have rather airy-fairy ideas about living in tune with nature under the pagan gods (as well as asking Zeus for peace, they put in an additional plea for rain) – again not something that *bona fide* paganism put much stress on.

More crucial, though, is what's missing from this religious revival. True, the worshippers last week poured a libation of wine and incense over a copper tripod. But where was the animal sacrifice?

As almost everyone who studies ancient Greek religion insists, the key centre of the whole religious system was sacrifice: it was the ritual of killing and sharing the animal that was, if anything, the 'article of faith' that defined the ancient community of worshippers. And it was through sacrifice (rather than ecology) that ancient Greeks conceptualised their own place in the world – distinct from animals on the one hand and the superhuman gods on the other.

Until these eager neo-pagans get real and slaughter a bull or two in central Athens, I shan't worry that they have much to do with ancient religion at all. At the moment, this is paganism lite.

Comments

Mary, Aristotle, *Phys*. 2.8 198b17–18, must have slipped your mind: 'Just as Zeus sends rain so as to grow the crops …' Precisely what this means (and whether A. himself believes it) is a matter of some debate, but it seems not unreasonable to think that someone might have a go at encouraging him to rain at the right time.

JAMES

You sound like you rather hanker after a good old-fashioned hecatomb …

And as for 'Ellenais', my favourite thing about the whole story was the alliteration from the Greek Orthodox spokesman, who labelled them 'a handful of miserable resuscitators of a degenerate dead religion who wish to return to the monstrous dark delusions of the past'.

After a lot of the stuff with which the C-of-E comes out, I just like hearing clergymen who aren't mealy-mouthed …

POSTBLOGGER

Does Mary realise that she is paraphrasing a remark of G. K. Chesterton's originally made, I suppose, about a century ago? I can't at the moment lay my hands on the original quotation, but he made a remark in one of his essays to the effect that 'some people say that paganism is returning: when Parliament is opened by the sacrifice of a white bull on the steps of Westminster Palace, then I shall believe that paganism has returned'.

DAVID KIRWAN

Where's the loo?

20 March 2007

Most Cambridge colleges 'went mixed' some twenty years ago. But they still preserve unexpected corners of male power and privilege. None of these corners is more irritating than the location of the female loos.

Imagine it. You're sitting in the SCR – that's the Fellows' common room – after dinner. You casually ask for the Ladies. The chances are that there will be a bit of a flap, while the equivalent of an AA route map and a compass is produced. It usually involves going out into the courtyard, through the rain, into the next court, up a staircase three doors on the left – only to discover a set of facilities which you know to be decidedly inferior to whatever is laid on for the men, and much less 'convenient' in almost every way.

Some colleges, to be fair, are a bit better organised; and my own, I confess, treats male needs with almost equal disdain. But the general rule seems to be that women's ablutions are lower down the pecking order than men's.

I have never really understood why single sex loos are necessary, anyway, in a place like a university (King's Cross station late at night is probably another matter).

Why can't we just share?

In my more paranoid moments, I strongly suspect that the answer has to do with men's urinals being one of the few remaining sites of exclusively male wheeling and dealing. Men will disappear for a pee in the middle of a meeting and come back, after a cosy chat in the loo, with the business fixed.

Women can't do that. Female toilets are strangely discreet places, for the simple reason that you never know who is locked in the cubicles – invisible, but capable of overhearing every word that's said. There can hardly be a woman in the land who hasn't learned her lesson on this one: bitching in colourful terms about a woman who two minutes later emerges to wash her hands.

This was something that repeatedly got Ally McBeal into trouble in that wonderful old television series. As the joke used to go: How do you know if you're an Ally McBeal fan? Answer: If you look under the toilet stalls to see who's using them before you start talking.

Surely it would be easier, and an imaginative blow for female power and equality, just to make urinals a thing of the past and put everyone in the same facilities. It's already common enough in the USA (in fact, Ally's loo was a 'unisex', as I recall). It's we Brits who have this illogical obsession with urinary segregation – to the extent that we are even known to make students use separate toilets from the staff.

… So what did the Romans do? you'll be wondering.

Well, domestic loos were something of a rarity. But the evidence from Pompeii suggests that, if they were present at all, the usual location was in the kitchen. There was convenient water supply and Roman assumptions about hygiene were rather different from our own. Better not to think too hard about the consequences.

Outside, and in places such as baths, they had an excellent line in splendid multi-seaters. Though whether these were also mixed sex we don't, I think, know.

I'd like to imagine that they were.

Comments

I don't think you need to worry, Mary. It's usually the case that men's loos are a very silent place. Engaging a fellow pee-er in conversation mid-stream is something of a taboo.

JAMES

James, I am delighted to hear it! Obviously, by definition, we cannot know the conventions of the loos of the other sex. But I'm still not wholly convinced that they don't exchange the odd 'I really do think Dr X is the best candidate' – return to the meeting and hey presto!

MARY

I am not sure what Mary means about male privilege in Oxbridge colleges. In my first year rooms at Oxford, I had to cross one quad for the loo and two for a bath.

OLIVER NICHOLSON

This reminds me of the famous riposte of Sir Winston's: when asked by his successor PM at the loo of the House of Commons why was he rather stand-offish, his reply was 'because you will nationalise anything big you see'. So much for the wheeling and dealing in the loo.

ARINDAM BANDYOPADHAYA

Anyone claiming it's taboo for men to talk at urinals must not spend much time in pubs.

MAX

Despite some fleeting suggestions of irony, your blog touches upon two matters of considerable moment and great contemporary concern. In a forthcoming paper on evacuation to be published in Vol. XXXVIII of *Studia Mathematicae Antiquitatis*, 2024 (3), I shall tentatively suggest that the fact that Archimedes' wife chased him along the streets of Syracuse vociferating 'You reek, You reek' constitutes incontrovertible evidence that in middle to late 3rd century BC Sicily it was in fact common practice to pee in the bath.

FRED O'HANLON

Do-it-yourself cremation

27 March 2007

Death tends to play a big part in a Classics degree. Ancient poetry and drama is full of murder, suicide, assassination, contested burials. Archaeologists love nothing better than a cemetery to dig up. At Cambridge we have a whole third year course on the topic, which covers death from every possible angle – from Socrates to Trajan's column (which, of course, to return to this contested subject, contained Trajan's ashes in its base).

One of the first things the students learn is that, with the exception of emperors, a few other dignitaries and the occasional new-born babies, Romans were always buried outside the city. Hence those roads like the Appian Way outside Rome, lined with tombs.

With a nostalgic image of an English village in mind (graveyard nestling next to the village green …), we tend to treat this as a slightly odd, unfamiliar practice. In fact, arrangements in modern Cambridge are strikingly similar. The crematorium is located outside the city limits, on the main A14 road towards Huntingdon.

Once upon a time this may have been a peaceful green-field site. Now the grieving friends and relatives are forced to negotiate one of the most accident-prone highways in the country (perhaps not all that different from the Appian Way in that respect). I dread to think how, on exit, they tearfully weave their way into the speeding lanes of trucks.

Black humour would suggest that this was a way of the crem drumming up its own trade.

When you hit 50, you find yourself at more funerals than weddings (or, to put it frankly, more of your co-evals are dying than getting hitched). Last Monday, I made my way up the A14 to the ceremony for an old friend who had died in her 80s. In fact, even though I know the route perfectly well, I actually missed the exit off the dual carriageway and had to take the next one and double back. So I didn't arrive in the chapel till the coffin had already been carried in.

As always, once I was there, I found myself thinking about the logistics of the whole operation (displacement activity, I guess). It's hard not to admire the seamless organisation – and the timing – which lets one grieving party out of the side door as another one enters through the front. Someone must spend their life planning other people's funerals with split second care – and just occasionally it must go embarrassingly wrong, with the wrong audience around the wrong coffin.

As for the clerics in charge, I'm a bit more ambivalent. On the one hand, I'm full of admiration again for anyone who can turn up and even begin to choreograph a fitting funeral ceremony in front of a group of people they don't know, many of whom are feeling more upset than they have ever been before.

On the other, I'm none too keen on some of the packaging. I don't just mean the impersonality that creeps out from time to time ('I never actually met Harry …', as the standard admission from the pulpit goes). It's more a question of the default Christianity that takes over unless you work very hard to stop it. Under this régime, even the most questioning agnostic is likely to be dispatched with a chorus of claims about their future bliss in paradise on the other side of the pearly gates. Given half a chance, the well-meaning cleric will even hint at deathbed conversion. 'I know that Sarah was not a church goer, but when I saw her in her last illness, I sensed a new spirituality …' Of course, a Christian ceremony is just fine for Christians – but not when it scoops up everyone else who can't actually claim another religion, or whose relatives don't have the instant presence of mind to explain exactly where their granny actually stood on the God question.

I'm pleased that I was canny enough to see this coming when my irreligious mother died. In a fit of bravery, over-confidence or pride looking for a fall, I decided to conduct the committal myself. The undertakers and the staff at Shrewsbury crematorium were a bit taken aback to start with. But funerals are not like weddings: anyone is allowed to do them, and say what they like. Once they saw I wasn't to be dissuaded, they gave me every help (right down to insider tips on how and when to push the button to start the coffin on its way).

I wish more people would take funerals into their own hands.

Comments

At least you have the option of being burnt in this country. In Greece it's been considered 'unchristian', so it was only after pressure from the EU and religious freedom groups that they passed a law this week to allow cremations.

However the crematoria have to be built and operated by town councils, so in the face of local (i.e. Christian) opposition I don't see one operating soon.

JOHN M

David Beckham's new tattoo – a classicist writes

18 April 2007

Becks has apparently decided that a move to Los Angeles demands a new tattoo or two. Not a feeling that the prospect of LA induced in me, but therein I suppose lies the difference between us.

Amongst the many designs now decorating the celebrity right forearm is what was originally a Latin slogan, here rendered in English: 'Let them hate [me] as long as they fear [me].' The idea is, or so I have read, to express something of Becks's anxieties about the transatlantic move, and his determination not to be battered by any adverse publicity.

I don't mind if they don't actually like me, so the message runs, but don't let them mess with me. Or, to quote 'a source': 'David … believes his tattoos can ward off negativity and help him battle adversity.'

The original reads in Latin: '*Oderint dum metuant*' (a nice example for you Latinists of the use of '*dum* as proviso, plus the subjunctive'). According to the *Daily Mail*, Becks first of all wanted the real Latin, but it was the word *dum* ('provided that/as long as') that caused the problem. Could it be taken as a reflection of the mental agility of Mr Beckham? Better perhaps to play safe by avoiding it entirely?

In fact, as any classicist must know, the word *dum* is only part of the reason why having '*oderint dum metuant*' or its English equivalent might be an own goal.

So far as we can tell, the slogan goes back to the second-century BC Roman tragedian Accius. Almost all of Accius' work is lost, but it is pretty certain that this phrase came from his play *Atreus*, and from the mouth of the title role itself. In ancient mythology and culture, this King Atreus was the limit case of tyranny and monstrosity – in fact, so much the limit case that he was the man who, so the story went, chopped up the children of his brother Thyestes, and then served them up to him in a stew (minus the hands and feet).

From then on, it became a catchword for the kind of ethics that a proper constitutional Roman deplored in a tyrant. Cicero and Seneca both regarded the sentiment as beyond the pale (hardly surprising, Seneca acerbically observed, that Accius' play was written during the dictatorship of the bloodthirsty dictator Sulla).

According to Suetonius, it was a favourite saying of the bonkers and wicked emperor Caligula – enough said? It was so well known that the wily emperor Tiberius seems to have parodied the phrase, pointedly. Confronted with some nasty popular squibs, he apparently responded, 'Let them hate me, provided that they respect what I am doing.' No rule of terror here was the (somewhat disingenuous) message.

So our celebrity hero is sporting a slogan that, for the Romans, its originators, was the instant identifier of the excesses of tyranny? Enough said?

Comments

Where's he got *'Pecunia non olet'* ['money doesn't stink'] tattooed?
XJY

It is strange that this quotation should have become corrupt so
early, so that even Cicero and Seneca got the wrong end of the
stick. Recent research into the writings of the mediaeval Alsatian
scholar, Hucbald the One-legged makes it fairly clear that the
quotation does not come from Accius' *Atreus* at all, but from his
work on agriculture, the *Praxidica*. In the opening to the second
section, Accius is talking about poppies and says *'odorant tum
metuntur'* [untranslatable Latin pun: ed.] – they give off a sweet
smell and then they are reaped ...

MICHAEL BULLEY

Don't blame Hadrian for Bush's wall

30 April 2007

President Bush has a strange enthusiasm for walls (strange, because that mother of walls in Berlin isn't exactly regarded as a stunning success). He would like to put, if not a wall, then at least a barbed wire fence along the almost 3,500 kilometre frontier between the USA and Mexico. And, unless Nouri al-Maliki manages to put the brakes on, there will soon be concrete walls between Sunni and Shia areas of Baghdad, to keep car-bombers out (or in).

Bush isn't the only one, of course. Israel is busy constructing its West Bank barrier, parts of which are 8 metres high, in concrete. Less well known is a wall put up in Padua in north Italy, as a 'crime fighting measure', around the high-rise Anelli estate. In fact the *Guardian* last week came up with almost thirty modern security walls, either built or under construction. One, the electric fence between South Africa and Mozambique, has apparently killed more people than were killed trying to cross the Berlin Wall.

The Great Wall of China may be one ancestor here. But the usual Western approach is to point the finger back, way beyond Berlin, to the emperor Hadrian. Regret these awful barriers though we do, is the line, there is a fine classical precedent in the second century AD with Hadrian's attempt to keep the nasty barbarians out of the Roman empire. That is, 'Hadrian's Wall'.

Another misuse of the classical past, I'm afraid.

Sure, the popular image of Hadrian's Wall is just that: cold, wet, Roman squaddies constantly patrolling the bastions, and periodically attacked by the native hordes trying to penetrate the homeland – unsuccessfully, of course, as the Wall was such an effective barrier.

It can't, in fact, have been anything like that, and archaeologists have been debating for decades exactly what Hadrian's Wall was for. The one relevant reference in classical literature ('he was the first to build a wall to separate Romans and barbarians') may look as if it supports the popular line. But it's written by a flagrantly unreliable late Roman biographer of Hadrian, who probably had no better idea than we do of what was going on in the second century AD.

And there are all kinds of problems with that approach. For a start, the Wall isn't anything like as powerful a defensive line as we tend to imagine. There are one or two spots where it looks very impressive (and those are where the publicity photos are usually taken). But when it was first built most of the western part was not that great masonry structure, but a simple turf rampart, which wouldn't have deterred most self-respecting barbarians. Besides, there are an improbably large number of gates (80) for a serious defensive barrier.

Some modern archaeologists think that we are dealing with a mechanism of surveillance, or with a means to control movement between territories, rather than an attempt to prevent incursions (maybe there was a cash levy on goods crossing the line ...?) Others think that it was more a way of establishing a line of communications from east to west, rather than blocking invasions from the north. Still others think that the main purpose was symbolic: Hadrian was one of those unwarlike Roman emperors who needed some military street cred; what better than a few miles of military masonry in the rugged province of Britannia?

But the bottom line is the way the Romans generally thought about frontiers and frontier regions. Despite the impression given by Hadrian's Wall (and by a few other places, largely in Germany) that they saw a linear divide between the empire and the barbarian world, the Roman image of the frontier was usually much more subtly nuanced. The empire shaded into 'foreign' territory across many kilometres that were a melting pot of cultural difference and often a hot-spot of trading and commercial activity. It was a question of frontier zones, rather than frontiers – governed partly by Rome, partly by a whole variety of non-Roman powers. Hadrian's Wall, whatever its function, was an exception.

President Bush and our other wall-crazy political leaders might learn from that.

Comments

Rome had all those soldiers up there in the middle of nowhere, with nothing to do. Someone came up with the idea: Why not build a wall? – just to keep them busy. After all, the Romans were always building something.

TONY FRANCIS

If the purpose of Hadrian's Wall was at least as much symbolic as practical (and I think there's a strong case for that), then it is a precedent for Bush's fence along the Mexican border, which is surely as much about being seen to be Doing Something as actually having any practical effect.

TONY KEEN

I'd go for a phrase like 'conspicuous demarcation'. Mary mentioned a lot of uses, and Tony adds the 'devil-finds-work-for-idle-hands' one, but of course the reason for all the soldiers being there in the first place is to demonstrate the presence of enormous numbers of troops available just to garrison a god-forsaken corner of the world like this. Hinting at thousands more to be mustered when needed.

XJY

Seminar power and willy-waving

5 June 2007

When I go to a lecture or seminar paper, I expect it to end on time. If it is billed for 30 minutes, and Professor X is still talking at 45, I feel very itchy. Likewise if what Professor X says is plain wrong, then I expect to say so (politely enough) in the discussion session that follows.

All this seems to me to be quite 'natural'. But actually, I've learnt, these reactions are distinctively British. Although at first glance academic seminars look much the same anywhere in the world (a group of people banging on about subjects that would leave most of humanity quite cold), they are in fact governed by all kinds of culturally specific rules.

When I first went to such gatherings in Italy, for example, I couldn't understand why the chair didn't just shut a speaker up when he (or occasionally she) was still in full flood 30 minutes after he should have stopped. And I couldn't understand why the rest of the audience tolerated rambling responses from the audience lasting almost as long as the paper, and often on a quite different subject.

It took me years to see that in Italian terms this was the whole point of the occasion. For here academic power was calibrated precisely according to how much of the audience's time you could grab for yourself. If your junior colleague spoke for 8 minutes, then you were losing out in status very publicly if you didn't take at least 10 for yourself. And so on. Aggressive chairing and timekeeping would not only be breaking the implicit rules of the seminar; it would be disrupting the very roots of the academic power structure which the seminar supported.

In the UK (or at least in Cambridge, which may be a particularly extreme version of the British case), things are much briefer and – to put it politely – more punchy. How often have I heard my colleagues coming out of a seminar, one saying to the other 'I thought you made a good point'? What 'good' means in this context is 'a comment that in two witty sentences completely demolished the whole paper of the poor visiting speaker and showed how much cleverer you were than her'.

I confess that I am becoming increasingly ambivalent about this kind of display. On the one hand, I grew up with it and am still half attached to its style. I remember as a young lecturer thrilling to the displays of wit and smartness which the then Professor of Ancient History, Keith Hopkins, would put into his responses to dull papers given by speakers. 'I have three reactions to your talk and the first is boredom' is a direct, memorable and (as I now think) memorably nasty quote. And I am sure that I am sometimes guilty of playing such lines myself.

On the other, it's fairly obvious that what's driving this kind of discussion is not an engagement with the topic of the lecture or paper delivered, but peacock-like preening. It's a very male set of responses (even when done by women). It is, as one of my female colleagues has aptly put it, an exercise in 'willy-waving'. Power games in a non-Italian form.

That said, the seminar style in the States leaves me feeling rather at sea, too. There are (as I found at Stanford) some examples of the British mode, but by and large everyone is seamlessly polite. It's not that they don't have strong views about the quality of the lectures they hear (as you discover when you talk about it afterwards), but round the seminar table, it's flattery all the way: 'Thank you so much for that masterly performance …'/'I learned an enormous amount from your excellent paper …'

To start with, it makes you feel very warm. But then you think: How would I know if I had done a really lousy lecture? Would my best friend tell me? Or is there a subtle code among all this eulogy that I just haven't mastered yet?

Comments

A colleague has a wonderful account of a Department Meeting where a woman faculty member said; 'OK chaps, dicks on the table', which may be what Mary is referring to. But there is a serious problem here: how does one react to a lousy paper? The UK 'interesting' is a helpful usage, and I once got mileage from confusing *Merkwurdig* with *Bemerkenswert* in German, though I lost all standing. Can we invent an international gesture (probably already to be found on Greek vases and in Terence mss.) for 'Could do better?' … Or, in a democracy ruled by the RAE and its collaborators, must all seminar papers be equal?

Q. H. FLACK

Italians asking questions: … Gilbert and George turned up one lunchtime at the British School at Rome to actually talk. At the end a guy from the *Messagero* made a longish rambling point (c.10 minutes), more or less in the form of a question. At the end George murmured, 'Interesting.' The first seminar I went to (in the late sixties) was given by Peter Brown, who even then was grooming himself to be a guru. There was no discussion or questions (how

could there be ?). Since I did not know what a seminar was, I
assumed that it was simply a lecture with a smaller audience.

ANTHONY ALCOCK

I have noticed expressions of power in who chooses to sit where.

In a small format seminar where 10–12 people are seated
around the usual configuration of tables the person who sits to
the first left or right of the speaker often wishes to dominate the
event. Interestingly, in a graduate student seminar setting, it is
often the weakest student in the room who also will choose to sit
next to the professor. I guess you could call it power siphoning …

The person who sits the farthest away from the speaker, at
the opposite end of the table, wishes to establish a rival center of
power as he or she considers himself to be a higher authority than
the speaker and will, of course, talk incessantly …

EILEEN

Howard Mohr's essential study 'How to Talk Minnesotan' shows
that the good people of Lake Wobegon have the true word Q. H.
FLack wants for disposing of such phenomena as inferior seminar
papers. It is: 'That's different', with appropriately Scandinavian
pitch accent on the initial word.

OLIVER NICHOLSON

It is very hard to generalise accurately about the US. At Cornell,
where I had my first post, Lisa Jardine and I were scolded for
asking sharp questions of a distinguished visitor who had given
a shoddy lecture. At Princeton, the Davis Center under Lawrence
Stone was the scene of many a public disemboweling. At Chicago,
where I studied, there is also a tradition of critical questions, but

quite different in style from those at Princeton. I'm sure the UK shows similar variations.

TONY GRAFTON

Presumably if you are the speaker and you suspect your host/audience of flattery, you can then start grilling them on precisely how they think your paper improves on the existing state of knowledge. Or is that to be eschewed for fear of being labelled a c*nt-flasher?

SW FOSKA

My ex-husband, a surgeon, goes to many international congresses. He told me how, in the US, going over your allotted time was not tolerated, and the chairperson would just switch off the microphone.

SARAH HAGUE

Resident in the US for near 30 years but having been educated in the UK, and growing up there in an 'academic' family, I agree completely; I grew up understanding that a concise dry wit was to be sought after – expressions of politesse that required parsing like UN resolutions were thought of as waffling hypocrisies. Having said that, intellectual disagreement was very rarely taken personally – which I find in the US, sadly, almost inevitable, however 'diplomatically' phrased.

Alas, in my experience there are few like the late Columbia don Sidney Morgenbesser: 'A famous Morgenbesser anecdote arose during a lecture by J. L. Austin in Oxford. Austin said it was peculiar that, although there are many languages in which a double negative makes a positive, no example existed where two positives expressed a negative. In a dismissive voice, Morgenbesser replied from the audience, "Yeah, yeah …"'

MICHAEL ROBINSON

While at the American Academy in Rome I had the opportunity to observe several national seminar styles at work, and at odds. The American scholars were particularly wary of audiences with a large German contingent … it opened the possibility of what they termed a 'shark attack.' They even coined a phrase – *tristedescophobia* – fear of three or more Germans in the room.

ROY

It has not been unknown for an overlong sermon to have an assisted termination from a cipher discovered on a pedal stop by an organist in readiness for the final hymn.

DR VENABLES PRELLER

Pompeii in Mexico

18 June 2007

My new project is to write a book on Pompeii which captures something about life in the ancient city. Books on daily life in the Roman world, with one or two honourable exceptions, tend to be disappointing ('Romans rose early and took a light breakfast' – you know the kind of thing). So why not try to go in through the one city we know best?

Besides, there is a huge amount of specialised new work on Pompeii that hasn't much impacted on books for a wider audience. They tend to make more of the vulcanology and its horrors ('their brains boiled') than life pre-eruption. In my book, Vesuvius will definitely not have the starring role.

The problem I have is not getting together some marvellously evocative material. I had, for example, no idea that a monkey's skeleton had been found among the bones at Pompeii. And I'm still curious about the cart ruts. The problem is being able simply to picture the street scene. I haven't been able to close my eyes and conjure up the living city.

That is, until I went to Mexico on a quick holiday from the Getty Research Institute in LA. As we drove from the airport on the first day through the backstreets of Oaxaca, I said straightaway: 'This is Pompeii.' There were narrow, paved main(ish) roads – intersected by unpaved, dirt-track cross streets. Low-rise shops and workshops, with wide doorways, line the streets; sometimes they have an upper storey, sometimes not. Every now and then, a larger and grander residential property emerged, with an impressive portal but an otherwise off-putting blank exterior. On the more populous streets, there were political slogans, too – not on posters or bills, but painted directly on the walls by obviously professional sign writers (and there were a good few old ones, which had clearly been painted over). Just like those Pompeian electoral '*dipinti*'.

When we got to the ex-village, now suburb, where we were staying, it was much the same. Grand houses, with peristyle gardens, lurking behind curtain walls, cheek by jowl with the local internet café or hardware store. The husband aptly compared our hotel to the House of the Faun.

The point, I reflected, was not that this place looked like Pompeii might have done. It was more that it seemed to share with the ancient world an idea of what (to put it in the jargon) 'urban space' was for, and the acceptable collocations between poverty and wealth, luxury and squalor. In London (or Los Angeles), the very rich tend not to live next to hardware stores.

The irony was, I discovered, that one of the painted wall slogans had already made a link to the Roman world. Not far from the hotel was the local library, with its name and an improving message painted on its façade. That message ran (in Spanish): 'Science and letters are the nourishment of youth and the diversion of old age.'

It's a quote from Cicero's speech *Pro Archia* (the defence of a poet): '*haec studia adulescentiam alunt, senectutem oblectant*'.

Is David Cameron a Narcissus (… Or, was John Prescott right?)

21 June 2007

Classical allusions have been flying in Parliament. David Cameron has likened John Prescott to the combination of Bevin and Demosthenes (a truly horrific mixture, even if it was meant as a kind of back-handed compliment), and Prezza has fought back with some Greek mythology: 'The Leader of the Opposition reminds me of someone, too. When I read Classics and Greek mythology at the Ellesmere Port secondary modern school, we learnt about Narcissus. He died because he could only love his own image. Yes, he was all image and no substance!'

The trouble is that the message of the Narcissus story isn't exactly about being all image and no substance. It's far nastier than that.

The version of the story we know best is from Ovid's *Metamorphoses*. It starts with one of those mysteriously dark predictions given, on his birth, to Narcissus' mother by the blind and gender-bending seer Tiresias. Narcissus, he said, would live a long life, provided that he did not get 'to know himself' (a puzzling reversal of the famous slogan displayed at Delphi which says that 'knowing yourself' is exactly what you should aim at).

Of course, the prediction comes horribly true. Narcissus grows up to be a real stunner, but far too proud to reciprocate any of the many advances made to him. That's where Echo comes in: she, poor nymph, wasted away to just a voice, pining for his affections. But another rejected lover had a more spirited response, and begged the goddess Nemesis for vengeance in a particularly ingenious form: let her make Narcissus fall in love with himself.

And so, drinking from a pool, he spots his own reflection and becomes instantly infatuated with what he sees. Unable to have his desire (for it was only a reflection), he too pined and died (and the narcissus flower grew up in that very spot).

But there's an earlier version of the story, too, which turned up on an Egyptian papyrus in Oxford a few years ago. Some of the basics are the same, but here it is men who are in love with Narcissus, not women. And instead of just pining away, Narcissus kills himself – and from his blood the flower grows.

My first instinct was to think that the Deputy Prime Minister was just plain confused with his Greek mythology. It's not that Narcissus simply is 'all image'. The sharper point is that he is in love with (the image of) himself.

But then I wondered if we shouldn't be giving Prezza's classical learning the benefit of the doubt. Maybe he was cleverly hinting at the theme of self-love – and even (supposing that he's kept up with Oxford version) a tinge of homo-eroticism. After all, there was no trick that ancient orators enjoyed playing more than accusing their rivals of effeminacy.

'La Clemenza di Tito': Mozart, the Colosseum and Yugoslavia?

25 June 2007

Just back from the fleshpots of Los Angeles (the hard-working fleshpots, I should say), I had the treat of a night at the opera – the final reward for some programme notes I wrote for the English National Opera sixth months ago. The chosen gig was Mozart's *La Clemenza di Tito (The Clemency of Titus)* at the London Coliseum.

I hadn't actually seen it or heard it before – and really chose it because I inferred (correctly but blindly) that it was about the Roman emperor Titus (79–81 AD, son of Vespasian and honorand of the famous arch in the Forum). It proved to be intriguingly weird in all kinds of way. The singers did a wonderful job, but a lot of the music sounded to us more like 'School of Mozart' than 'Mozart.' And the storyline was about as implausibly convoluted as *opera seria* can get.

It featured, on the one hand, a scheming Vitellia, daughter of the short-lived emperor Vitellius, who wants to become empress of Rome – to avenge her father's fall from power (marriage to Titus being the quickest route). And, on the other, the emperor himself, wanting a consort to replace his beloved Jewish Berenice, whom he has just sent away to assuage popular Roman opinion which would only accept a native Roman wife for their emperor. The search is predictably dogged by rival suitors, covert plots and outright rebellion in the city. To all of these adversities Titus responds by blessing his rivals and pardoning the disloyal. Hence the title.

But the fascination for a classicist was the set – on either side of the curtain. The performance was a revival of a David McVicar production which turned Titus' court into an austere, if somewhat chilling, amalgam of the Ottoman and the Japanese palace (Topkapi meets the Chrysanthemum Throne). We couldn't decide if the long-skirted, broad-belted imperial bodyguard were meant to evoke janissaries or samurai. It was in this elegant, uncluttered imperial surrounding that Titus repeatedly forgave his various enemies and rivals.

But I wondered if McVicar had ever reflected on the ambience in which the Coliseum audience would be watching the show. For the Coliseum, built early in the twentieth century, beats any theatre in London for its extravagantly Roman design. Taking its cue from what we generally now call the Colosseum, the interior is festooned with references to Rome and the Roman arena – chariots of lions, laurel wreaths, gladiatorial weapons.

Look up from the auditorium and you'll even spot a painted version of the *velarium*, or canvas sun shade, which used to keep the worst of the heat off the audience at the Roman games.

And who was responsible for building and opening the (original) Colosseum? None other than Titus, of course. So, on either side of the curtain, we had two very different versions of Titus' image. On the stage, the calm and forgiving ruler – too forgiving for his own good. On the audience side, the bloodthirsty monarch, who presided over those murderous games (take a look at Martial's book of verses commemorating its opening if you want to know how murderous) without so far as we know a jot of clemency.

But what was it all about?

An excellent essay in the programme did very well in trying to relate it to eighteenth-century debates on kingship and 'enlightened despotism'. Was the emperor above the law? Was Titus right or wrong to pardon a conspirator who had actually been formally convicted by due process of law?

I couldn't help thinking that there was a very obvious target in one of the most famous (in Mozart's day) works of Roman philosophy – Seneca's *On Clemency*, a quotation from which featured in the programme. Seneca was the tutor of the emperor Nero and wrote this treatise to his pupil advocating the use of clemency and forgiveness in imperial policy (strikingly unsuccessful in its short-term objectives, it must be said). The whole plot of *La Clemenza* could be seen as a riposte to this. For here Titus' only weapon is forgiveness – and it leads to one disaster after another (from personal unhappiness to the burning of the city). Maybe, we were being asked to reflect, Titus just once should have said, 'No pardons today.' A total capacity to forgive is, in other words, no less destructive than the reverse.

Quite what the rest of a largely enthusiastic audience made of it, I'm not sure. Things weren't helped by the fact that for most of us over 40 the Italian form of Titus – that is, Tito – has a whole set of other political resonances.

In the men's loo, my husband overheard an unsettling snippet of conversation: 'I don't quite see how this fits into the rest of the history of Yugoslavia.'

He thinks it was a joke.

Index linked?

4 July 2007

I should have known better. But when my publishers asked me if I wanted to prepare the index of my new book myself, or have them get a professional, I instantly said that I would do it myself.

The main reason was that I have, in the past, seen some really dreadful, so-called 'professional' indexes (the kind where you are enticed by an entry to – say – Virginia Woolf, only to find, on looking it up, some such phrase as 'Born in the same year as Virginia Woolf, our hero …'). I also self-importantly thought that only I, as author, would be able quickly to identify the underlying themes that were most worth signalling (so making the kind of index that transcends the simple computer word search and, at its best, gives a parallel intellectual structure to the book for an attentive index reader).

There was a hopelessly optimistic side to this, too. I thought that at this last stage I would positively enjoy reading the whole typescript through, post-partally, for one last time, then sitting back to reflect on the main index-able themes. I was going to create an index-to-die-for.

I should have known better. For a start, I've done this before – and should know that those days of leisurely re-reading in an armchair never quite materialise; it's always a rush. I had also read the long correspondence in the *TLS* at the end of last year, all about the pitfalls of indexing. That should have reminded me.

As it turns out, I've spent five days on it (for 440 pages of book), and actually I am not unpleased with the result. But it hasn't been remotely fun doing it.

First of all, there's the re-inventing the wheel problem. If I was a (good) professional indexer, I'd already be up-to-speed on this. But in my apprentice-like state, I have to think through the basic questions of categorisation from the bottom up. My book is about the Roman Triumph. So do I have hundreds of entries saying things like, 'Triumph, origins of', 'Triumph of Lucius Aemilius Paullus', or 'Lucius Aemilius Paullus, triumph of' … or what? (Actually what I decided was to have a big subheading in the index in bold caps, saying **TRIUMPH** … and all those subheadings underneath, 'origin of', 'chariot in', 'deification and' … and so on. Hope it works.)

But just as tricky was what to leave out. This is the Virginia Woolf problem. There are references all over the book to (for example) the historian Dio Cassius. Does each one need an index link? ('As Dio emphasises, the triumph was …') Well, no – but how do you decide? The principle has to be: would any reader looking up a reference to Dio through my index actually want to arrive at this page? Which is fine in theory, but I can tell you that at midnight, and half a bottle of wine later, it can prove hard to make up your mind.

Then there are the jokes. I've loved index jokes ever since my friend Keith Hopkins slipped one into the index of his *Death and Renewal*. It ran, 'Methods, authentication from fragmentary evidence, *passim*' – with other entries for 'speculation', 'tautology' and 'deviants, punished'. I flirted with a few ('Ancient historical study, self-indulgent futility of, *passim*'; 'Triumph, Roman, fun to study') but rejected them – mostly on the grounds that I couldn't imagine enjoying them in two months' time – let alone ten years' time, when I hope the book will still be around. So I settled for a parody of, and homage to, my much missed friend, 'Facts, fragility of, *passim*'.

Which just happens to be true as well.

Comments

From Isaac Casaubon's diary, 2 February 1614 (OS): *Hodie ab instituta cogitatione rejectus sum ad curandos indices, quos ille corruperat, qui onus in se susceperat.* ['Today I was diverted from the inquiry I had begun to preparing my indexes – which the man who had taken on the job had ruined.'] And 5 February: *Et illiberales istae curae de indicibus me plane occupant ... Tu, Domine, miserere. Amen. Hodie absolvi indicem auctorum et descripsi inter varias curas et impedimenta insigni usus diligentia.* ['Indeed those vulgar concerns with indexes are altogether distracting me ... Have pity on me Lord, Amen. Today I finished the index of authors and transcribed it among various concerns and hindrances, taking tremendous care about the process.']

There are some continuities in the lives of serious scholars ...

TONY GRAFTON

When you & that Grafton chap get to edit the *Oxford Book of Grumpy Scholars Complaining about Indexes*, don't forget Syme's preface to his *Tacitus* monograph: 'The task has been long and laborious (for all that ostensible drudgery can be sheer delight). It has been hampered by various delays and vexations. Nor, in making the written text fit for publication and compiling the vast index, can aid or alleviation be recorded from any academic body, from any fund or foundation dedicated to the promotion of research in history and letters.'

SW FOSKA

You've had it now, M. Beard. You will get SUCKED IN. I've indexed two of my own books – largely because I thought it would (a) be fun and (b) gave me an excuse to buy the brilliant Cindex indexing software – and then did a friend's book (Louise Foxcroft, *The Making of Addiction*) & in each case it was a bit like doing one of those join-the-dots puzzles: what emerged at the end was a delightful meta-text revealing themes that neither I nor Dr Foxcroft had seen in the main body of the book. I discovered, for example, that for an avowed atheist I was remarkably engaged with God ... And I think the highlight (and Triumph) of my life was being invited to give the keynote speech at the American Society of Indexers conference in Pasadena ...

The comparison between computer-generated and your own indexes will be fascinating. Indexing is a cognitive and critical enterprise & scope for fun. Bet you're importuning friends and colleagues to let you index their books before the year's out. 'Go on. Let me. Pleeease. Just one, then I'll quit ...'

But doing your own index isn't without pitfalls, even if, like me, you're allowed to make slightly surreal entries. I find on my current book I am writing some passages thinking, 'Gosh, this is going to come up well in the index', which may indicate a cart/horse category error ... but it's fun all the same.

MICHAEL BYWATER

Foska, I couldn't quite get the tone of the Syme. Is he pissed off that he hasn't benefited from any fund or foundation? Or is he proud not to have had anything to do with that new-fangled rubbish? Or, I guess, both?

And by the way, the excellent Prof. Grafton and I are about the least grumpy scholars I know!!

As for Bywater … I do recommend him as a nobel laureate of the genre. (And his is the only index in which I've ever seen an explicitly flattering reference to myself … as in 'Beard, Mary, better scholar than I'll ever be …' … or do I misremember?)
MARY

Mary, I think you are right about Syme, he is being both grumpy and smug. But careful – Foska was proposing you and Grafton as editors, not contributors.
SW FOSKA

How to order a coffee in American

6 July 2007

My trip to Mexico was another linguistic challenge. Pride coming before a fall, I thought that if I could read Spanish (… well, Spanish books on Roman religion, at any rate), I could speak it too.

In fact, that wasn't too far from the truth. Although the husband accused me of just speaking loudly in a bastardised form of Italian, I was quickly pretty confident in saying, *'Dos margaritas, sin sal'* ('Two Margaritas without salt', as we have it), and the like. The problem was understanding what on earth was said back.

This is almost always how it is with foreign languages. It's easy enough to muster enough German to say: *'Wie komme ich am besten zum Bahnhof.'* But, unless you can understand 'Turn sharp right at the abattoir, then half left just after the war memorial, and you'll see it on the other side of the roundabout', you might just as well not have bothered.

But it's not just in foreign languages. A few months in the USA made me think that a lot of successful human communication, even English to English, depends on knowing in advance what your interlocutor is likely to say back to you. It means knowing the script in advance, in other words. Try to order a coffee in Los Angeles, and before you get a nice steaming latte, you will have to have given a series of quickfire answers to a whole load of unexpected and quite un-British responses: 'Regular?', 'Half-and half?', 'Long or short?' More

than once I was left as baffled as if the barista had been
speaking a half-understood GCSE language.

It made me wonder if there were two versions of English
learning text books the world over – the UK, and the US
version.

And what would one of those 'at the coffee shop' learning
dialogues look like in each?

UK English:

Waitress: What can I get you?

Mary: A chocolate muffin and a coffee.

Waitress: Black or white?

Mary: White, please.

Waitress: Be right with you.

US English:

Waitress: Hello, I'm Cindy and I'm your waitress for this
afternoon. In addition to what you see on the menu, we
have a special of delicious wholemeal English scone and
full cream. What can I get you?

Mary: A chocolate muffin and a coffee, please.

Waitress: Would you like the organic chocolate muffin, or the
regular?

Mary: Organic, please.

Waitress: Our organic cocoa beans are from Guatemala. Is that
all right for you?

Mary: Don't you have anything from Africa?

Waitress: Not organic, I'm afraid.

Mary: OK, Guatemalan is fine.

Waitress: And the coffee? Latte, cappuccino, espresso …?

Mary: Latte, please.

Waitress: Half and half?

Mary: No, I'd prefer no-fat, thanks.

Waitress: Long?

Mary: No, regular would be fine.

Waitress: That'll be right with you, and if there's anything else I
can get you …? Have a nice day.

I'm not claiming that one of these is better, more nuanced,
brisker than the other. It's just that I'm still not quite sure I've
mastered version 2.

Comments

One of the curious aspects of US descriptions of food items is
the insistence on attaching the adjective form of the country
of origin to them: Albanian split peas, Bulgarian onions and so
on. Your example of an exchange in the cafeteria (and my own
limited experience of eateries in Manhattan) makes me wonder
if all Americans are subjected as children to a good sound drilling
in stasis theory (rhetoric): let's thrash this out before we go any
further.

ANTHONY ALCOCK

That's nothing … you should go to a Tim Horton's in Canada
where you will hear all sorts of people ordering anything from an
extra large double double (i.e. double sugar, double cream), which
sort of makes sense, to an extra large regular (one cream, one
sugar), which doesn't. Fortunately I am a denizen of Starbucks and
they know my order (triple grande sugar free vanilla non fat latte
and a doppio espresso) so I don't have to repeat it.

DAVID MEADOWS (ROGUECLASSICIST)

When I asked for a burger in a McDonalds in Manchester, it was
presumably a corporate policy devised by an American which
prompted the young female assistant to ask, 'Is that a meal?' It
was sheer grumpiness, my blissful ignorance of 'McDonald speak',
and memories of introductory philosophy tutorials 30 years ago
discussing category error, etc., which prompted me to reply 'What
an interesting question! It depends, I suppose, on what you mean
by "a meal". My reply was not appreciated, and the subsequent
exchange became rather heated. I now know that 'Is that a meal?'
in that context means 'Do you wish to have a drink and French
fries with that?'!

JAMES R

That's odd. I asked for a hamper in Fortnum and Mason's with no
clue as to its contents and was told that a hamper meant 'Do you
wish to have Christmas pudding and the finest Stilton with that?'
So much for the wrapping!

CHARLOTTE

A minor philological quibble: If Cindy said, 'I'm your waitress for
this afternoon', she certainly wasn't speaking in standard US idiom.
To American ears, that sounds awkward. Typically a waitress uses
the future tense and says, 'I'll be your waitress …'
  Oh, and this, too. Unless you accidentally left out the indefinite
article in the phrase 'delicious wholemeal English scone' (or
forgot to pluralise 'scones'), that utterance, too, is completely
unidiomatic. We would speak of 'a scone', 'the scone', or 'scones', but
never just 'scone'. Is the word 'scone' used as a plural in the UK,
the same way we here in Arkansas say, for example, that we're
'hunting possum'?

K. D. C. JONES

Now that we're quibbling, I'd take it a bit further: our American Cindy, if she works in a shop that sells organic products, would most likely use gender-neutral pc speech and say: 'I'll be your server today.'

EILEEN

At least Cindy did not use the loathsome neologism 'waitron' (whose earliest *OED* citation is from 1980, where it is made to rhyme with Hilton – yuckyuckyucky).

OLIVER NICHOLSON

What is Big Brother doing in Durham cathedral?

27 July 2007

I have just got back from overnighting in Durham. I had a gig talking to a splendid Summer School – 100 schoolkids and adults giving up a week of their vacation to learn Latin and Greek (and some heroic teachers giving up a week of theirs to teach them).

Shamefully, I hadn't been to Durham ever before. The somewhat grumpy taxi driver who picked me up at the station didn't really see why I was bothering.

After all, he opined, Durham was just like Cambridge – only smaller.

He was wrong, of course. They might both be overrun with students ('posh' students, as he put it). But Durham's got the cathedral … which is where I headed in the half hour I had before supper yesterday.

I didn't have a guidebook with me. But one of the advantages of being married to an art historian is that you always have the equivalent of your Pevsner at the end of the mobile phone. So I quickly found out that I should be looking at the ribbed vaulting and the Treasury.

In fact by the time I arrived, the Treasury was closed and choral Evensong had started. So I did my duty on the vaulting and stuck to the west end – which included a terrific Father Smith organ and a Lady Chapel featuring the (nineteenth-century) tomb of the Venerable Bede. This is inscribed with some ghastly Latin doggerel: *'hac sunt in fossa Bedae Venerabilis ossa'* < roughly 'In the tomb underneath these stones/Of the Venerable Bede you'll find the bones'> As an eminent Latinist friend has explained to me, this is a medieval 'leonine hexameter' and it does have the advantage of being simple enough for even the beginner to translate. But, all the same, it must be making the learned Bede turn in his ... *fossa*. Touchingly, yesterday there was a 'best wishes' card to the saint displayed on top, from a class of children at 'St Bede's' school.

I haven't plodded round many English cathedrals for years (though I have now discovered that the East Coast Main Line gives you a fantastic ringside view not just of Durham, but of Ely, Doncaster and York, too). When I do set foot on consecrated ground these days, it's much more likely to be in Italy or Greece – and for no more holy purpose than to see the Caravaggio in the third chapel on the left. That said, for anyone (believer or not) brought up in the traditions of mainstream Anglicanism, there remains something comfortingly familiar about the whole thing. I walked in at what was obviously the Second Lesson of Evensong – Peter had just denied Jesus again and the cock was about to crow. It was a script I already knew.

But as I looked round, the place turned out to be 'familiar' in a much more surprising, more institutional and more disconcerting way. And much less like the cathedrals I remember. For a start, they had obviously got caught up in disability legislation – so every possible set of steps was kitted out with a ramp (I accept that when I come to be in a wheelchair I may be grateful for all these ramps – but I hope that even then I will prefer to have the building left in peace and a couple of burly guys to give me a lift).

Then I found that they had latched on to the idea of the mug-shot photo gallery at the way in, just like every university department in the land. For some reason the Bishop himself wasn't included in this (was he too grand?), but everyone else it seemed, was there – from the Dean and Chapter, down to the vergers and the Development Director (so it really WAS like a university …)

But the final straw of familiarity for me was the CCTV ('CCTV operates in this cathedral' ran the notices, just as they do in college). What, I wondered, was Big Brother trying to spot? Someone nicking the candlesticks? Inappropriate behaviour in the Lady Chapel? Or was it the religious police, homing in on those not joining in with the hymns or saying the Creed with enough conviction?

Give me back some of the mystery, I thought.

Comments

At least the Father Smith has not been replaced with a device enabling its simulation by digital reconstruction, though such equipment is useful for practice purposes.

DR VENABLES PRELLER

Durham Cathedral may or may not be the resting place of St Cuthbert. He had been the bishop of Lindisfarne, which is now a ruin. There were many miracles attributed to the Bishop Cuthbert before his death in 687. He was buried in the cathedral of Lindisfarne. Eleven years later, the coffin was opened and St Cuthbert was reported to have been incorrupt. The coffin was removed several times due to invading Norse, and other warring factions. It was finally placed on September 4, 999 in the church which would become the Norman Durham cathedral. William the

Conqueror requested to view the body in 1069. The local bishop refused. In 1104, several local bishops disputed the condition of the saint's body. The coffin was opened and the body was reported to be in perfect condition. Henry VIII sent several doctors to destroy the body in 1537. When they opened the coffin, they found the body incorrupt. The coffin was filled with gold and gems. In the process one of the legs was broken. The doctors could not bring themselves to destroy the body. Benedictine monks re-buried the relic in 1542. The grave was opened in 1827, where the remains had skeletised. The mass vestments which were placed on the corpse in 1104 were still recognisable. There is a legend that the Benedictines secreted the body to a safe place after the incident with Henry VIII, and eventually lost track of where it was. Or, perhaps the skeleton is St Cuthbert, who remained incorrupt for 850 years. Plenty of reason for both mystery and CCTV.

TONY FRANCIS

Durham makes me think not so much of cross-rib vaulting as of Jacob's words after his dream: *'non est hic aliud nisi domus Dei et porta caeli'* ['this is none other than the house of the Lord and the gate of heaven']. Was the exhumation of S. Cuthbert's body in 1827 actually not undertaken by the Dean and Chapter precisely to disprove the rumours (put about when Roman Catholic Emancipation was in the air and many Irish RCs were going to Co. Durham to work in the mines and on the railways) that S. Cuthbert was hidden away at the Reformation? There was also a scientific excavation in *c.* 1890, and I think that it was at that date that the remains of the original 8th century carved coffin, which had travelled all the way from Lindisfarne via Chester-le-Street to Durham at the time of the Vikings, were taken up and stored (in the triforium). They were not reassembled, so I was told, till the

young Ernst Kitzinger came to Durham as a refugee from Nazi
Germany in the 1930s. There is an immense OUP book on the
relics of S. Cuthbert from the mid-1950s. The conference of 1987
marking the 1300th anniversary of his death has been published
(edd. G. Bonner, D. Rollason and C. Standliffe) and contains loads
of info – I may remember wrong (I could not afford the book!) but
I think little of it would support the secret burial theory mentioned
by the erudite Dr Francis. This was easily the most moving
academic conference I have ever attended.

OLIVER NICHOLSON

If you had turned up half an hour before dinner in your wheelchair,
though, the burly men would probably have gone home and you
would have not got to see the cathedral at all, mystery or no
mystery.

KATHARINE EDGAR

Marvelous article, marvelous comments, God bless England!

MATTHEW KLUK

Are A levels (still) dumbing down?

16 August 2007

As if to make it very clear that the answer to that question was a resounding 'no', the QCA (the Qualifications and Curriculum Authority) took out a full-page advert in some of today's papers. It congratulated all those students getting their results and quoted some of the questions they had had to answer.

The question that was read out on the morning news – from Psychology A level – was 'Describe and evaluate the contributions of the Psychodynamic Approach and the Cognitive Approach to society'. Cor, we were meant to think, that's hard.

It was, of course, something of a hostage to fortune. For a start, it may look gobsmackingly arcane to you and me, but turn to the A level board's specification for that paper and it is exactly what the students should have prepared themselves for:

Students, it says clearly in the syllabus, should be able to distinguish 'between approaches/perspectives in psychology, including … the psychodynamic approach, the cognitive approach and the physiological approach'.

So it wasn't exactly a wild card.

Next, it was just one part of a 90 minute paper, which – bearing in mind the time taken reading the paper and making your choice of options – would be answered in something like 20 minutes, which hardly gives time for much intellectual nuance. And, according to the examiners' reports, also published today, it wasn't even all that well done.

Here's some of what they had to say:

'Both approaches should have been considered, but some candidates only focused on one of them, which limited the marks available. The question asked for contributions to society, therefore theoretical contributions were only appropriate if they led to practical outcomes, e.g. theory of psychoanalysis and therapeutic techniques. Many candidates gave large amounts of irrelevant detail in this essay, for example, lengthy descriptions and evaluations of research studies to support applications, where only the identification and findings were needed.' And so on.

This isn't of course exactly what is meant by dumbing down. And in fact the strictures of these examiners may point in the opposite direction. The problem is not whether the kids are working hard (of course they are – and probably very much harder than we used to). It's the 'tick box' element to the marking that is the killer, and the sense that there is a range of points which have to be included to get the top marks – rather than the open-ended essay-style intellectual exploration.

I know of at least one A level examiner who has given up because he was forced to mark down candidates who wrote really intelligently about a subject but didn't give the points that were demanded by his 'marking criteria'.

When they get to university the hangover of this is still horribly apparent. Students will press you to say what kind of class you think their essay would be given. If you respond 'a 2.1', their next question is likely to be, 'So what have I left out that would get me a first.' As if getting a first was simply about fulfilling all the assessment criteria.

But tub-thumping about standards is a bit of a thoughtless response to all this. The sad thing is that the tick-box style of marking is an almost inevitable consequence of the very proper attempt to democratise A levels. It's all very well thinking that the open-ended intellectual essay style is what should be rewarded. But what do you do if you go to a school where they don't know the rules for that genre? Isn't it reasonable for you to expect to be told what you would need to do to get an A?

Perhaps even more pressing is the question of the examiners themselves. In the old days, when A levels were a minority option, you had a small group of experienced (and, no doubt, underpaid but devoted) examiners. You might trust them to make reasonably independent judgements about a kid's essay (and, in any case, the numbers were small enough for them to be checked up on). Our recent mad fixation with formal assessment has more than quadrupled the numbers of examiners that are needed – the demand being such that in some subjects trainee teachers are used to mark the most important tests in a child's career. So, of course, we have to generate firm rules and fixed criteria, simply to train and police the examiners.

The real question isn't whether we are dumbing down. It's what on earth we think all this examining is for. If it's for choosing the brightest, it's a blunt, time-consuming and inefficient instrument indeed. But maybe that's not its point – and we should be thinking of quite different ways to do that.

Comments

Just to remind Your Oxbridgeness how extra marks for adventurous answers preserves the *status quo*. If you belong to a group that you believe is discriminated against then you stick closely to the conventional criteria for marking, as otherwise you

can expect to be slammed. But if you know that you belong to
a favoured group – and especially if you come from a privileged
background and a bad mark wouldn't cripple your future – why
then you can afford to offer a daring submission that may win big.
And so we end up with a system where those awful conscientious
girls and those foreigners with their strange intense ways can
be sneered at because they don't get Oxbridge firsts because
'they lack that special something'. What they lack is confidence
in a system which they believe is stacked against then – after all,
people like them don't get so many firsts. And so it perpetuates.

JANEY

Janey's response … assumes that there is an either–or option
to solving the problem: either daring/adventurous/special or
conventional/conscientious.

Climbing Everest or taking tea with the Dalai Lama ('as Dalley
said to me last week …') can be done by anyone with access to the
preconditions. What conditions and stamps the underprivileged
masses is their lack of access to the preconditions for getting good
exam results – regardless of how the exams are set and assessed
…

In a crappy society, you get a crappy educational system. In a
contradictory society, you get elements of good among the bad.
Mary is desperately trying to separate the pearls from the turds in
her work. But she's stuck in the cesspool, so to speak.

XJY

Blimey, you would think blogging was an exam judging by some
of these scripts. Janey's point is valid, and Xjy's criticism of it
doesn't stand up. 'Interesting' is often used as a codeword for
'conforming to the marker's gross prejudices'. The student should

be given a clear idea of the rules, but this rarely happens. Being told something of the content doesn't make it easier. If I publish a specification for an exam in flute-playing which says 'Candidates must be able to demonstrate shit hot flute playing skills' and the 2-hour exam paper, with one question, says 'Play the flute brilliantly for 2 hours', that's still quite hard … I'll probably get a C minus now for poor structure & insubordination.

Foska simply cannot understand Prof. Beard's (far from unique) impatience with students' desire to be told, on being given a 2:1 grade, 'So what have I left out that would get me a first?' Compare cricket: this English game is alleged to be rife with covert ideological normalisations of abnormal hierarchical arrangements, and yet the rules are clear. If a player hits the ball over the boundary rope, he scores four. Nobody thinks him an ingrate or cheapskate if he asks how it would be possible to get more; he would be clearly informed that he has to hit the ball over the boundary without it touching the ground, and he will get six. Foska cannot see how that diminishes either the game or the pedagogical experience.

Or to put it another way: if I fail a driving test I want to know why.

SW FOSKA

I take Foska's point. But – having failed my driving test more than once – I think that the reasons for failure were more complicated than those given. The sheet I was given may well have marked the three point turn, but the real reason was that I just couldn't drive How do you put that on a tick box?

MARY

How would you have felt if, upon failing, you had asked what the matter was and received the response, 'Well, you just can't drive.'

Where on earth do you go from there? It's vague, unhelpful and essentially just a cop-out. Perhaps he only ticked the 'three-point-turn' box, but at least that gives you SOME idea of what to work on.

You may be applauded for condemning the 'tick-box' system that prevents talented (not 'gifted', the word is a misnomer) students from achieving top grades or forces lesser students into an unhelpful tick-the-boxes-and-get-the-marks mindset, but don't ever criticise a student for asking how they could have scored higher. Answer them!! Is there a reason they didn't get top marks? Necessarily there is, so explain it to them.

Getting a first IS simply about 'fulfilling all the assessment criteria'. They might not be as simple or as obvious as 'mention Thucydides', but undeniably they exist – if only in the mind of the individual examiner. Explaining to a 2.1 student how they can work toward a 1st is at the heart of the educational process, and if you can't do that then I would offer that the whole thing is a waste of time.

RUPERT

Turned up a bit late for this discussion but still ... I got full marks in my A2 level Latin unseen this year even though I managed to translate *'superiore aestate'* as 'at the higher tide'. They gave us *'aestas'* and I declined it at the time and worked out it wasn't possible ('earlier in the summer' – got it later in the afternoon and nearly broke shin kicking myself). There were lots of other mistakes I can't remember, too. I felt cheated, to be honest – all very well giving bonus marks for good English but incorrect Latin is incorrect Latin and there was no way it deserved 100%. Not that I sent it back for remarking or anything, you understand.

JENNY

Esperanto, Welsh and the language wars

20 August 2007

Could Esperanto save the world? When I was a kid I did learn a few words of this proto-global language, invented (as a gesture to intra-planetary understanding) in the 1880s by the doctor-cum-linguist, Polish-cum-Lithuanian Ludwig Lazarus Zamenhof. He had, it was said, toyed with the idea of bringing back Latin as the world's second language (that actually would have been easier for me). But instead he decided to construct his own, making it nicely simple, with no pronunciation traps and easy, consistent rules.

It ended up as an odd hybrid of Latin and German, with a smattering of French and Italian (not to mention a bit of ancient Greek '*kaj*' is 'and' in Esperanto, after '*kai*' in Greek). So '*plena*' is 'full', and '*plenplena*' is 'very full' (Greek reduplication, I suppose). And '*mal*' is the negative: '*ami*' means 'to love', '*malami*', 'to hate'. Get it?

It was through my Dad that I ventured into Esperanto a little. He, in the spirit of his times, saw Esperanto as a weapon in Moral Rearmament – as well as a blow to Welsh (which, as we lived in Shrewsbury, crept incomprehensibly through our letterbox on the phone and electric bills).

I didn't meet Esperanto again till the 1990s.

That was when a friend of mine was writing a wonderful biography of J. E. B. Mayor, Cambridge Professor of Latin (and, as it happens, educated in Shrewsbury, as most of them were). It turned out that one of Mayor's numerous obsessions (he was amongst other things a born again vegetarian) was Esperanto.

And, I learned, he gave the address to the Esperanto Society Congress in 1907.

I didn't think about this again until I picked up the Cambridge evening paper, where there was a marvellous piece of local history on this congress, by Cambridge chronicler Mike Petty. I hadn't realised quite what a big deal this conference was: it had involved a sermon in Esperanto in the University Church and in the Catholic equivalent; Oscar Browning had starred in a version of the *Pickwick Papers* in Esperanto; and the *Evening News* had carried a cartoon of the police being taught Esperanto to deal with the trouble-makers. There was also a photo of an Esperanto agitprop stall in just the same place in the Market Square where you'll now find the animal rights activists.

Esperanto now seems (sorry, Esperantists) faintly silly. And having a nice little European-style language as a *lingua franca* seems hopelessly out of touch. That said, there is something rather cheering about the unbatterable optimism of those who think that they can right the world's wrongs by inventing languages. It's rather like George Bernard Shaw's new English phonetic alphabet.

Or, come to think of it, it's like the new phonetic letters introduced by the enterprising Roman emperor Claudius to make Latin itself more transparent. His letters were actually used for a while – and they've even recently been recognised to the extent of having their own form as characters on the Unicode computer text.

Wouldn't he be pleased?

Olympia (almost) burns … but Paris survives

27 August 2007

First let me apologise for writing about the antiquities of ancient Greece, when so many people have died in the terrible fires – probably almost a hundred casualties altogether so far. It reminds me a bit of the 'bombing' of the Parthenon in 1687, which everyone now laments as the loss of a great building, forgetting the hundreds of women and children killed in the process.

But, conscience apart, even as I'm writing, it is not entirely clear what exactly has happened to which ancient sites in the Peloponnese.

The good news seems to be that the Greek and Roman remains of Olympia have escaped (and a lot of them, let's remember, are of Roman imperial date and not from the fifth-century BC well-springs of democracy at all). The Greek Archaeological Service is very good on disaster planning, and almost certainly its fire protection devices, as well as the brave fire-fighters and a dose of good luck, played their part in keeping the site safe.

But the news reports have tended to concentrate on Olympia alone – when, in fact, there are any number of sites round about whose loss would be almost equally troubling in archaeological, even if not symbolic, terms. I think here of the temple of Apollo at Bassae on its romantic hillside (the temple itself is now covered with a strange, almost post-modern tent). We still don't know whether this has made it. Let alone the much less well known temple of the 'Great Goddesses' at Lykosoura in the valley below. And that's before we start to think about the Byzantine churches gone up in flames.

At this point I begin to feel grateful for the dispersal of antiquities around the museums of the world.

Suppose Olympia and its museum had actually gone up in smoke (and fire quickly turns marble to a little pile of lime). At least some of the sculptures of the key temple of Zeus would have been safe in the Louvre. And if the temple at Bassae had been destroyed, then it would turn out to be a good idea after all that the sculptures from its frieze were in the British Museum in London.

This is not an argument about the quality of care these monuments are given whether in Greece or abroad (and almost all guardians of the Greek heritage – Greek or foreign – have something to be embarrassed about). It is more the 'stuff happens' problem. Nature sometimes seriously messes up. In other words, like it or not in aesthetic or political terms, there is a very practical point to these Wonders of the World being split up.

There's also an argument here for the old-fashioned plaster cast gallery. If the Olympia sculptures were to be destroyed in both Greece and France, then you would still be able to find a perfect set of replicas in the cast gallery of the Museum of Classical Archaeology in Cambridge (and in other plaster cast galleries the world over). Half a century ago many of these cast collections were themselves threatened with the (sledge-) hammer. Now we are a bit wiser about our fragile hold on the masterpieces of the past – and the need to protect them in a variety of guises.

Comments

Not a popular post! Almost all of the many comments fell somewhere on the spectrum between upset and offensive, ethnocentric and vengeful:

'What about scattering the British Crown Jewels around the world …?'

'Shame on you, OPPORTUNIST.'

'UP YOURS.'

'fuck!! of!!!!!'

'In the pure tradition of her ancestor Lord Elgin.'

'When we were building the Acropolis, you were living in caves.'

'They were Greek and they will remain GREEK for ever in GREECE.'

… and so on.

10 things you thought you knew about the Romans … but didn't

30 August 2007

After the flood of angry comments about the last post on the Greek fires, let's try some happier topics. A fellow blogger suggests that we classicists tend to keep too many secrets about the ancient world to ourselves. So let me share a few.

Here are 10 things you thought you knew about the Romans but didn't. 10 myths about the Romans exploded … !

1   Julius Caesar's last words were '*et tu brute*'
Well, only in Shakespeare's version of the assassination. Probably our best ancient source is Suetonius and he records the words as (in Greek) '*kai su teknon*' – or 'you too my child'. What this means, in fact, isn't so clear. If it has a question mark, it smacks of quizzical, dying desperation. Give it an exclamation mark and it becomes a threat ('they'll get you too, kid …')

2   Rome was built on seven hills
Some serious miscalculation here. Palatine, Aventine, Capitoline, Janiculan, Quirinal, Viminal, Esquiline, Caelian, Pincian, Vatican. That's 10 for a start. Though it all depends, I suppose, on what you call a hill.

3   Romans had 'vomitoria' to be sick in between courses at lavish dinners
Sorry. This is an old one, But *vomitoria* were the exit routes which spewed people out of the amphitheatres.

4 Roman men dressed in togas

OK, sometimes they did. But it was very formal wear – and it's a bit like saying 'Englishmen wear dinner jackets'. Actually, you'd have seen all kinds of dress on the Roman street, from tunics to trousers – and, just to confuse things, prostitutes in togas.

5 Nero fiddled while Rome burned

Not if you mean that he sat around ineffectually twiddling his thumbs while the city went up in flames. Actually what Nero did was fiddle in another sense: he played the violin (or so it was said).

6 The plebeians were the Roman poor

OK, Romans, just like us, did sometimes use the word 'plebeian' or 'plebs' for the 'great unwashed' (literally, 'sordida plebs'). But in the strict sense both 'plebeian' and 'patrician' were old hereditary divisions of the Roman people. These may once have signalled the poor/powerless versus the rich/powerful. But by the time of the later Republic there were enormously rich plebeians – like Marcus Licinius Crassus, the plutocrat who famously said that you couldn't be counted as rich if you couldn't raise your own private army.

7 Gladiators said 'hail Caesar, those about to die salute thee' before each show

This favourite phrase is actually attested only once in classical antiquity – and not at a gladiatorial show. It was apparently spoken by the participants at a mock naval battle laid on outside Rome by the emperor Claudius.

8 When the Romans finally destroyed Carthage in 146 BCE, they ploughed salt into its soil – to make it completely barren

This is slightly trickier ground, but there is no ancient writer who says this. It's a view that got common currency thanks to an article by B. Hallward in the first edition of the *Cambridge Ancient History* – and he gives no ancient reference.

9   The Romans were much smaller than us
Depends on who you mean by 'us'. The skeletons found in Pompeii and Herculaneum actually suggest that the Roman inhabitants were on average a bit taller than the modern Neapolitans.

10   Hadrian built his wall to keep the barbarians out of the province of Britannia
Only if he was a military idiot. A good proportion of it is built just in turf anyway, which wouldn't have deterred many self-respecting barbarians. Even if the rest was in stone, it is now thought much more likely that the whole thing was administrative (for customs levying perhaps) – and to help east–west communications.

And that's only the first ten!

Greek treasures and global treasures

4 September 2007

I only wish that many of those who exploded at my post on the Greek fires had read it in English. That's not meant as a criticism. I can read modern Greek just about well enough when I need to, but given the chance to read an English translation I'd always take it. So I can hardly object to others relying on the account of my views on the *Ethnos* website.

The trouble is that it was a bit of a travesty of what I actually wrote. For the record, I'm NOT advocating that the Greek heritage should be distributed wholesale abroad for 'safe-keeping'. I am simply arguing that there *is* something to be said for some dispersal and replication. Part of the reason is an entirely practical one: it's the 'Wills-and-Harry-never-in-the-same-plane' sort of principle.

And for those of you who thought that I was being decidedly insensitive – to say the least – in even raising these issues at a time like this ('to make such ill comments/suggestions at the time of national crisis in Greece, it just shows the type of person that you are'), please note that I did start the post with an explicit apology for just that – and, for good measure, with a sombre reflection on the hundreds of Ottoman women and children killed when the Parthenon went up in smoke in the seventeenth century.

All the same, the intensity of the responses took me aback a bit. It wasn't just the abuse: 'fuck!! of!!!!', as one commenter put it, or 'UP YOURS MY DEAR..', in the (slightly) friendlier words of another. It was more the bigger debate about the role and preservation of cultural heritage revealed by many of these hard-hitting reactions.

Several of the comments raised the issue of the English Crown Jewels. How would I feel if some of them were sent to New York (as John M. wondered)? Well, the true answer is that I would feel perfectly OK about it – and I half suspect that even now they're not all in the Tower anyway (on the same 'Wills-and-Harry' principle). To put it more positively, I actually feel pleased when I go (for example) to the Metropolitan Museum in New York and see those English country house rooms, once in Oxfordshire or wherever, now reconstructed transatlantically. I like the idea that visitors, who come in from the extraordinarily different world of Fifth Avenue, should find themselves reminded of 'my' culture.

The other side of this coin is that I cannot agree with the idea that works of art have some necessary and natural 'home'. Nor do I think that those who now live in the place where ancient masterpieces were created (whether they are the direct ethnic descendants of the creators or not) are the only people in the world who could possibly be qualified to care for them or to speak on their behalf. So I find it hard to respond to the question: 'WHO GAVE YOU THE RIGHT TO HAVE AN OPINION ABOUT OUR HERITAGE?' (whatever 'right' means in this context). And I could not agree that only modern Greeks can properly look after ancient Greek antiquities. That's a claim which would not be true for the antiquities of any country in the planet – Greece, the UK, the Sudan, India, you name it.

I can think of few worse strategies of cultural planning – particularly for a globalised world – than one which demands that all works of art stay in the geographical area in which they were made. That's partly for reasons of safety, but partly too for the worthy aim of cultural interaction.

Now hang on before you reach for the 'send' button. I know that there are crucial issues of power and politics here. While I fully support the notion of a universal museum, it hasn't escaped my notice that in reality these so-called 'universal museums' tend to exist in western Europe and the US – not in Ghana or Burkina Faso. Which is to say that the universal museum and imperialism have been, historically, at some level connected. It is also clear that it is easier for a country that has been a net 'gainer' rather than a net 'loser' out of these processes to feel culturally 'generous'. It's clear, too, that some objects are more singular and symbolically important than others (sending the Eiffel Tower to Australia would be quite different from sending, say, Monet's *Waterlilies*). All the same, the basic principle of sharing seems a good one.

It still is tricky with material monuments, though. And that's partly the problem of their materiality itself. We can all 'own' Shakespeare or Mozart or Seferis. The claims of Stratford-upon-Avon do not affect the possibility of sharing the Bard's plays as widely as you like. Plays and poems and operas are infinitely extendable, unlike marble – which really is destroyed by fire, despite some optimistic assurances to the contrary. How we can share *physically* monuments which are *ideologically* shared by the whole world is a problem we haven't yet begun to resolve.

Upstairs at the brothel

11 September 2007

I am now in Naples for seven days doing some serious hard graft at Pompeii: my last good look at the site before I write my book on it.

One of the Pompeian places that is sure to feature somewhere in this book is the Brothel. Now that the famous House of the Vettii is closed to the public, it is this that is the tour guides' hot spot, nicely restored with Danish money a few years ago. On the ground floor, it consists of five little rooms, each with a fitted stone bed – plus a single loo, though no running water.

What makes it 100% certain that it is a brothel rather than (say) a cheap lodging house is the decoration (a lot of more or less unimaginative bits of painted erotica above the doors to the 'cells'). And, of course, the graffiti: all over the walls are scrawled boasts and confessions, along the lines of 'I fucked Glyce/I want to fuck Glyce/I fucked Glyce for tuppence'.

Hardly surprising, I guess, that it attracts streams of visitors. And hardly surprising that the site authorities enter into the spirit of it a bit. Some wag, no doubt worried about the effect of light on the paintings, has posted 'No Flash' on the notice outside.

But what I've always wanted to know is what happened upstairs.

The Brothel is a two-storey building, and the upstairs is shut to the public. Some books tell you that there were more rooms for sex workers there. Others claim that it was where the girls slept or took a break between clients. Until this week I hadn't had permission to go and see for myself.

What you actually find is a neat stairway (with a loo at the bottom) plus five more rooms. One is a rather nice, and nicely decorated, large saloon; the others smallish chambers of some sort. There were no obvious cooking facilities. So if anyone lived here, beyond fruit and bread, etc., and some hot snacks and the ancient equivalent of a cup of tea cooked up on a portable brazier (lots of those are found in the city), they would have eaten out.

So what was this suite for? Well, it could hardly have been more 'working' rooms. At least, there was not an erotic painting in sight and no graffiti at all, so far as I could see.

So what then?

Well, maybe the girls' quarters, with four bedrooms (for how many workers?) plus a recreation area. But it was hard to resist the idea that the nice big room was where that stock villain of Roman comedy, the pimp or '*leno*', hung out and counted his takings, and lived in some style (even if minus a kitchen).

Or maybe, as one of our party pointed out, we were still being too fanciful. Given the multiple use and multiple occupancy of most domestic space in Pompeii, this could equally well have been the flat of someone who just happened to have the address 'Above the Brothel'.

And as for the girls? Just as likely that they slept on (or off) the job.

How many academics does it take to buy a coffee maker?

21 September 2007

Are academics hopelessly incompetent boffins who couldn't run a chip shop?

I usually get very cross about this silly myth. In fact, I have a US bumper sticker on my office window which says (words to the effect of): 'The trouble is that the people who ought to be running the country are too busy teaching school.' If nothing else, it amuses the passing tourists.

But just occasionally, we (or, let's be honest, I) do seem to live up to the myth.

Take, for example, the idea that the hard-working Fellows of Newnham might have a coffee machine that would make good coffee 24 hours a day in their Senior Combination Room (that's what we call our 'common room') – replacing the Thermos jugs that are now put out three times a day, and quickly lose their freshness, taste and heat.

This subversive idea was first mooted about three years ago. Specifically, some super-brain came up with the idea that we might have one of those Flavia machines, which makes you a very nice cup of coffee from a little foil sachet.

But there were closely argued objections from two sides.

First there was the eco lobby. Some of the Fellows were far from happy with the environmental wastage caused by all those sachets. Then there were the taste police, who thought that this bulky modern machine was an inappropriate intrusion into our lovely Victorian Combination Room.

I had some sympathy with both of these. I cannot imagine who could possibly have invented a coffee system that left such a large quantity of foil and plastic behind. Nor do I think that the machine matched our Combination Room very well, which is by far the prettiest in Cambridge. (I'm biased, but most of the others are in men's club style, whereas ours is 'ladylike' and is kitted out with lots of delicate 'ladylike' chairs – not made for bulky blokes, who tend to look a bit silly in them.)

But neither of these objections seemed to me to outweigh the need for 24-hour coffee on line.

These arguments rumbled on for a couple of years (sic). But when I became the President of the SCR in March (an entirely honorific post, aimed exclusively at making the Fellows' lives better, sending them flowers when ill and improving books to their newborns), I decided to get some action, with the valiant help of the Catering Manager and the Domestic Bursar. The good news was that most people agreed that we could put the machine in an interconnecting room next to the SCR, which didn't have the same aesthetic qualities. Even better, we had found a slightly different machine that did Fair Trade coffee.

A perfect compromise. And the new machine was duly installed in the cupboard in the interconnecting room, our consciences safe in the knowledge that we were helping the producers in the Third World.

Problem solved, until we tasted it.

It was indeed Fair Trade, but it was also *instant* coffee. At which point a different wing of the taste police came out of the woodwork: their perfectly reasonable point was that when they said they wanted 'good' coffee, they didn't mean instant.

So what do you do with a newly installed (expensive) coffee machine that makes coffee that no one wants to drink? Well, the first answer was to find another group in the college who did and go back to the first idea of the environmentally unsound Flavia machine (the eco warriors having admitted defeat).

The only trouble is that the Flavia machine is about an inch too big to fit into the space, which means that either we have to have the maintenance department alter the cupboard, or we have to swap our new machine with the Bursar's older, and slightly narrower one. For he of course – one of those bulky blokes who look faintly silly in the little chairs – has had an environmentally unsound Flavia machine in his office for years.

An everyday story of academic folk.

(Before everyone writes in to complain about what a waste of public money we are, etc. etc. … let me assure you that this is only what we do in our 'spare time'.)

Comments

Three years to buy a coffee maker? Would that you academics had been in charge of the British government the last three hundred years. You might just now be contemplating pillaging half the world and you would not all be suffering from post-colonial angst. I never had an actually drinkable cup of coffee in Cambridgeshire, due largely to too much roasting of inferior beans, and too much heat during and after brewing.

DON S

MARY BEARD

Elegiacally:
Quae tibi, Barba, bonum profundet machina potum? Flavia non est, nec Gaggia, sed Magimix! ['What machine produces a good drink for you, Beard? It's not Flavia nor Gaggia – but Magimix?']
MICHAEL BULLEY

Thanks for bearing with this little story. There is a happy ending – for we now have a Flavia machine successfully installed, to the pleasure of all concerned. I am told (happily) that the Junior Combination Room has now got a Flavia too. The housekeeping dept put in a bid for the Fair Trade and everyone seems delighted.
MARY

At another SCR in Cambridge not far from Newnham, we have a delightful, and small, machine which grinds fresh beans on demand and effortlessly produces perfect Italian coffee in various sizes depending on the user's preference. Occasionally cryptic messages appear on its display asking to be cleaned, or descaled, or for more fresh coffee beans to be added, but for the most part it does its thing extremely well all on its own at the simple push of a button, and the coffee is the best I've ever had in an SCR in Cambridge. I thoroughly recommend it … you will have to make a tour of Cambridge colleges to find it!
ANON

Why does your Bursar have a coffee machine all to himself? Just take his!
DEX TORRICKE-BARTON

The sex secrets of Kennedy's *Latin Primer*

25 September 2007

A friend e-mailed me at the weekend on the subject of
Kennedy's *Latin Primer*. He had come across an old article
in the *Guardian* by the no less distinguished Valentine
Cunningham, suggesting that the 'Memorial Lines on the
Gender of Latin Substantives', which form an appendix to the
Primer, were a 'camp semaphore' – in other words, a cover for
a series of steamy references to pederasty. It was an argument
about Kennedy I had missed.

For those who do not number Kennedy among their
bedtime books, these 'Memorial Lines' are a series of jingles
to help the young learner remember which Latin nouns are
masculine, which feminine and which neuter. ('To nouns that
cannot be declined/The neuter gender is assigned …', as one
of the more memorable examples goes.) To judge from my
father's memory up to his deathbed, they were once drilled
into the heads of the young. Already in my day they seemed a
bit quaint.

Cunningham was really interested in the re-use of the
jingles by Benjamin Britten in his version of *The Turn of
the Screw* (no problem with the camp there). What caught
my attention was his claim that, by a very careful choice of
examples, old Kennedy himself – whose *Revised Primer* came
out in 1888 and is still going strong (even if we don't do the
jingles much any longer) – encoded a very similar message.

My first instinct was to scoff. But after a bit of work, I
wasn't so sure.

The particular example Cunningham, and Britten, were interested in was this (you'll have to say it out loud to get the flavour):

Many Nouns in *is* we find
to the Masculine assigned:
amnis, axis, caulis, collis,
clunis, crinis, fascis, follis,
fustis, ignis, orbis, ensis,
panis, piscis, postis, mensis,
torris, unguis and *canalis,*
vectis, vermis and *natalis,*
sanguis, pulvis, cucumis,
lapis, casses, Manes, glis.

Kennedy translates all the Latin words he uses here in a sober fashion: 'river, axle, stalk, hill, hindleg, hair …' Cunningham points out that a surprising number of them had other meanings. *Clunis* ('hindleg' for Kennedy) is anus; *caulis* ('cabbagestalk') can also mean prick; *follis* ('bellows') is slang for scrotum. And so on.

For Cunningham, this was 'school-master funnies' for 'other Latin masters in the linguistic know'. I checked all this out with the *vade mecum* of Latin smut, J. N. Adams's *Latin Sexual Vocabulary* (which is what I imagine Cunningham had done) and found myself agreeing that an awful lot of this Latin did have a decidedly sexual second meaning.

A bit more work brought to light an article replying to Cunningham – by Christopher Stray, who knows more about Benjamin Hall Kennedy (Head of Shrewsbury School and Regius Professor of Greek in Cambridge) than any man alive. Stray poured cold water on the whole idea. For a start, Kennedy was born more than a century before Adams

investigated Latin sexual slang – and the dictionary he would
have used (Lewis and Short) – also still going strong) doesn't
register many of these *doubles entendres*. Besides, Kennedy was
a productively married man, with a son and four daughters
(two of whom, Marion and Julia, effectively wrote the *Primer*
that goes under their father's name – as Stray himself has
shown). If he translated raunchy terms into bland euphemism
('hind leg' for 'anus'), that was just Victorian prudishness.

Fair enough, and I am loath to take a different line from
Stray. But I still have a feeling that there is here no smoke
without fire. Kennedy's Lewis and Short dictionary may have
turned its back on quite a lot of smut, but it still recognises
caulis as '*membrum virile*' (and, in any case, I bet that the
acute Latinists of the late nineteenth century knew more than
what was in their dictionaries). And the fact that Kennedy was
married with kids is no proof at all that he wasn't well into the
pederastic culture of the period.

Besides, the more you look at it, the queerer it gets. It
doesn't take much to see another word lying behind Kennedy's
'*panis*'. And – taking a look through the other 'memorial lines'
– it is strange, to say the least, that all the dodgy words seem to
cluster in this particular verse on 'the Masculine'.

But don't let on, else they'll try to ban it.

Comments

In the *Classical Association News* (June, 2004), there is a letter
from one of Kennedy's great-great grand-daughters, who
underlines the fact that the rhymes were written, not by Kennedy,
but by his daughters, Julia and Marian. She adds that the idea that

these ladies might engage in paedophile innuendo via a grammar book is ludicrous. The balance of probability makes you think she is right.

MICHAEL BULLEY

'What is this that roareth thus?/Can it be a motor bus?/Yes, the noise and hideous hum/*indicat motorem bum*' was frequently recited by our retired Indian Civil Service headmaster (Indian in this context refers to location rather than nationality).

DR VENABLES PRELLER

Apropos bawdry and Latin grammar, do you know the epigram, attributed to Janus Secundus (1511–36), which is repeated by Casanova in *Memoirs, Vol. I*, Ch. 2?

Dicite, grammatici, cur mascula nomina cunnus, Et cur femineum mentula nomen habet.

(Say, O grammarians, why c**t is a masculine noun and p**ck feminine.)

Casanova claims it was posed to him as an 11-year-old boy by a quizzical Englishman, to whom he wittily replied:
'*Disce quod a dominis nomina servus habet.*'

('Learn that the slave takes the name of the master.')

PL

Orientalism ... or, what's in a name?

1 October 2007

On the front door of what was the Faculty of Oriental Studies in Cambridge, I have just spotted a new notice. Next to the stern warnings about not leaning your bicycle against the windows (a hopeless prohibition in Cambridge) is the following equally stern announcement: 'Name Change. We are now known as the Faculty of Asian and Middle Eastern Studies.'

I am sure that this has been the subject of long discussions. And I can see why they wanted to change. The word 'Oriental' now reeks of unacceptable 'orientalism', a nastily Western construction of any culture slightly to the east: decadent, effeminate but at the same time slightly menacing. (It's what the Greeks felt about the Persians, and the Romans in their turn about the Greeks, and so on westwards.) How, for a start, do you explain to a group of new first year undergraduates what an 'Oriental' Faculty is all about, and why it doesn't exactly mean what they might think it does? More to the point, how do you get them, in the first place, to apply to something with a name like that?

It's a bit like having 'Women's Studies' being called the 'Department of the Second Sex'.

All the same, I can't help feeling that it might have been more courageous and confident to sit it out with the old name. There would, after all, be some good company in that project. The Oriental Institute in Chicago shows no sign of turning itself into an Institute of Asian and Middle Eastern Studies.

And the School of Oriental and African Studies likewise seems happy enough with the title.

Wouldn't the cleverer strategy have been to try to reclaim the adjective 'Oriental' as an acceptable label again?

There are all kinds of example of this sort of problem. One recent commenter on this blog took me to task for using 'BCE' instead of 'BC', and I must say I think he had a point. I've tended to fall into this politically correct habit recently. But, no, BCE doesn't honestly seem any less 'Christian' in its emphasis than the old BC. If BCE stands for 'Before the Common Era', then (unless you change the counting system) isn't it simply admitting that Christian time IS the Common Era? And why should that satisfy any other of the world religions?

In my defence, I'd like to say that I haven't given in with the word 'pagan' – which I continue to use of traditional Greek and Roman religion, despite the fact that it was a disapproving Christian coinage hardly ever used by 'civic polytheists' (as we're supposed to say) themselves.

I haven't got my head entirely in the sand here. It's not that I think that the precise words we use are unimportant. But being blown by the political wind is not always the best political course of action. Isn't it better, and smarter, to reclaim the language of oppression? Look at the word 'black'. When I was a kid, you were told off fiercely if you were ever caught using it. Some version of 'negro' was the order of the time … which would now sound like a terrible bit of colonialism. The same is true too for 'queer'. When I was a student, it was enough to get you thrown out of the college bar. Now we all use 'queer theory'.

So, wouldn't it have been smarter to rebrand 'Oriental', not change the name into a temporarily acceptable periphrasis?

Comments

If the Orient, with its fascinating mysteries, is to be banished, what is to become of its nearer cousin, the Levant, one may wonder?

DR VENABLES PRELLER

Cambridge is of course merely engaged in slavish imitation either of the British Library (Oriental & India Office > 'Asian and African Studies Reading Room', c. 2005) or of Liverpool Arts Faculty (School of Archaeology, Classics & Oriental Studies > 'Sch. of A., C. & Egyptology', 2004) … The problem is not that the category 'Oriental' is not tainted, but that any alternative categories are of course equally open to knowledge/power manipulation. 'Levant' is just a French (via Italian) word for 'Orient' = rising.

SW FOSKA

Oriental is probably a better name here – who the hell decides what is the Whole East and in relation to what? and then who gets to be Far East and who Middle East and who Near East?

XJY

Tips for new students – from an old don

8 October 2007

The first week of term has ended, and our new students have just gone through the increasingly absurd ritual that is 'Freshers' Week'. I don't much mind the old-fashioned rites of passage that many of them organise for themselves: a bit too much alcohol and getting off with the wrong bloke to huge, but temporary, embarrassment all round. It's the ridiculous quantities of 'information' that we now feel obliged to impart.

They have lectures, workshops and leaflets on safe cycling, safe sex, how to write an essay, how to recognise meningitis, what plagiarism is, how the library works (in triplicate), how to deal with budgeting, how to have a good time without it getting in the way of the 2.1 of your dreams – and that's before they have even met their Director of Studies, received their work schedule or been to a lecture.

We must be mad. In the rest of our teaching lives, we are only too well aware of how much information the average highly intelligent young person can possibly absorb in an hour. At the beginning of term we simply ignore that. Though you only have to look at the behaviour of many of our first years on their bicycles to see that the safe cycling advice falls on deaf ears. Luckily, for most of them, experience teaches that one.

So why do we do it? It's partly unthinkingly well-meaning, and it's partly 'tick box' again, I fear. Do you explain to your students about AIDS/plagiarism/loan management …? asks some higher authority (whether the government or the students' union). Yes, sir, we can reply.

Left to myself, I'd cut it back down to a speedy hour or so.

But what would you say, if you could give them just one piece of advice?

Obvious: GET A DIARY. That's the single piece of advice that would lead to most benefit, efficiency, good work routine and happy living over the first year at 'uni' (as they now say). You would be amazed to discover how many students try to manage a complicated timetable and routine without one. Overall, more classes are missed by simply failing to write down the time and place in a little book (or even a BlackBerry) than by laziness or whatever.

After that, it's a bit more difficult to know what to put first. But I would go next for TAKE CARE WITH YOUR FACEBOOK. Yes, it's a wonderful medium of new communications. But your lecturers may well have registered, too, you know. So when you say (*pace* my last point!) that you couldn't turn up to your supervision because you were sick – when you have just posted 67 new photographs of that excessive party at which you had such a good time, they will know!

Finally, TREAT YOUR LECTURERS AS THE HUMAN BEINGS THAT THEY ARE. I get really fed up with being treated as some kind of teaching automaton, programmed to deliver information on Roman history come rain or shine … no feelings involved. On numerous occasions (… oh dear, back to missing classes again) students have apologised for not making a supervision a few days before with a cheery 'Sorry I didn't turn up, I wasn't well'. You don't just fail to turn up for a dinner invitation because you're ill: you get a message to your host in advance. Same courtesy for us, please.

Comments

It is both scary and wonderful to know that you have some of the same problems with your students that I have with mine at a US two-year college. So, from Cambridge on down, students are students, eh?

PHILOSOPHERP

The only thing I remember from my Freshers' Week was the Domestic Bursar holding a paper towel up in the air and telling us not to flush them down the toilet, but feel free to use them to pull our hair out of the shower plugholes.

JENN

The only thing I can remember from our Freshman's pep talk by the Dean was the utterance: 'You will have to matriculate, of course – don't worry, it won't make you blind.' I did wonder why no one else laughed. Poor fellows, maybe nobody had told them.

OLIVER NICHOLSON

How am I doing on Amazon?

19 October 2007

Most people go into Amazon to buy books: easy shopping, and it would be an entirely admirable enterprise, if it wasn't systematically killing all our local bookshops. Authors, though, sneakily visit Amazon to check how their books are selling, to plot their progress up (and down) the Amazon sales rankings – the bit that says '#47,543 in books'.

Actually, there are some odd things about this calculation. I was rejoicing the other day that my new book on the Roman Triumph (soon to appear in the UK) had reached number 2 in the Amazon.com (that's the US site) rankings … but in the niche subcategory of 'General Geometry'. (Quite how it got classified as 'geometry' beats me, but I guess it felt nice even so.)

But what every author wants to know is how many sales does it take to get you zooming up the Amazon ranks. I've always suspected that we were dealing with single figures here. But proof came the other day when the husband decided to buy 4 copies of his own book on icons, which seemed almost as cheap, and a lot easier to obtain from Amazon than from the publishers. The result was that he zoomed more than 250,000 places up the rankings.

Then there are those innocent customer reviews. Are they all written by real punters, or by the author's paid-up friends or enemies? Is it like those suspiciously frank hotel reviews on TripAdvisor ('Quite the best hotel in Beachville and far better than the awful Hotel Sunny next door')?

Just occasionally the reviewer confesses his or her bias ('Happy declaration … I live with the author'). But mostly we are left to guess whether these usually pseudonymous critics are the author's best friend, lovers or publishers or not. Frankly I suspect (though couldn't possibly prove) that big publishers have a small team of Amazon reviewers enthusing over their new books under the banner of 'Jeremy in Cambridge'.

A life in the day of a don

22 October 2007

I've had several emails asking what on earth do you dons do. When I tell people that my main formal obligation is that I am asked to give 40 lectures a year, it usually produces some such reply as 'Surely you meant *week*?' … and then howls of disbelief when I say, 'No, *year*.'

Actually, 40 lectures per year or not, the workload in term time amounts to a more than 12 hour day, 7 days a week.

The best I can do is give you an hour-by-hour account of one typical day last week. This is not in the spirit of complaint – because actually I love the job. But there are a few misapprehensions about our leisurely life that need to be put right.

OK, so let's take last Wednesday.

Work started at 7.00 a.m., with three long student essays to read and comment on. True, on another day I might have marked them the evening before. But I had spent most of Tuesday evening giving a practice job interview to a young colleague, and when I got home I read one of my graduate students' work – and that took till 1.00 in the morning or so and I just couldn't manage the essays.

I biked off to my Faculty at 9.00. The journey takes 20 minutes, as I'm a bit more sedate than some, but I managed to think about my upcoming lecture on the way. I ought to have done a bit more thinking when I arrived, but instead I had a meeting with one of my college colleagues about plans for student teaching – and I just about had time to photocopy an extra sheet for the handout, before the lecture at 10.00.

So at 10.00 I was talking to 120 first years about the Persian Wars and Orientalism. How many had read any Edward Said? None (but this was the group who had done much better on the map test than the previous year, so I half forgave them).

At 11.00 I had an hour with the PhD student whose work I'd read the evening before. Then at 12.00 one of my MPhil students came to talk about the seminar on Roman freedmen he is due to give in a couple of weeks' time.

So I ended up being late for the weekly meeting of our nineteenth-century history project (12.30–2.00), partly because I went via the Buttery to get a sandwich to eat on the hoof. We were discussing two pre-Darwinian texts on female beauty – fascinating stuff, but I had to slip out before the finish in order to get back to college at 2.00 for a two hour supervision on Roman religion with a group of three second-year undergraduates, whose essays I'd read first thing in the morning.

At 4.00 there was just time to look at the mail and some of the 50 or so emails that had come in since I'd last switched on, before I had to bike off to the station to get the 5.15 train to a college *alumnae* event in London. On the way, and on the way back, I got through one article submitted to a journal that I help edit and I read the papers for some job interviews and a Faculty Teaching Committee meeting that were both happening the following day.

Home on the 9.52 and getting back just before 11.30, I dealt with the backlog of emails and started to read the big chunk of work sent by another PhD student, but by 1.00 in the morning I was fading fast and went to bed – intending to be at work again by 7.00. (I nearly made it but not quite.)

And yes, I had – I confess – by then consumed rather more than the 1 unit of alcohol now recommended for us middle-class professional women.

Comments

Isn't it interesting how Oxbridge academics are never asked about any working time rules, or work out our actual hourly rate of pay?

At present I am seriously considering dissuading people from an academic career: the hours are long; recognition abysmal; pay poor (our students earn more a year or so after graduation); apparently pension contributions may be increased leading to a real-terms pay cut; administrative duties overwhelm and the one reason we choose the career, research, is always pushed on to the back burner. Frankly, in Cambridge all of my junior colleagues and I typically only manage to support ourselves by virtue of having a better-paid partner.

This sounds unfair and I love the research and the teaching (barring the exceptionally illiterate undergrads with whom one is occasionally confronted), but how the University plans to recruit and keep the best staff at present is beyond me. We seem to be relying on reputation (and the cachet that brings to academics) alone.

JS

I'm sure JS is right that Oxbridge academics are especially busy, having college tutorials as well as lecturing (on the other hand, terms are shorter). And certainly academics are badly paid (me included). But it's misleading to say that 'Frankly, in Cambridge all of my junior colleagues and I typically only manage to

support ourselves by virtue of having a better-paid partner.'
Plenty of people (incl. in the expensive South-east) earn less than
academics, and still manage to survive … And other employers
(including other universities!) don't sweeten the pill of bad pay
for new employees with so much subsidised accommodation, food
and drink, etc. as is provided by (many) Oxbridge colleges. My
girlfriend is a Cambridge academic. Is she going to have to leave
me for a City millionaire?!

RICHARD

My five favourite Roman classics …
that we have lost

29 October 2007

Classicists can be a miserable lot. When such a rich array of ancient Greek and Roman writing has survived, you'll still find them lamenting about what has been lost.

Most of the ancient literature we still have, we owe to the efforts of medieval monks who eagerly copied and preserved it. They didn't do a bad job. True, there are some oddities. Has it ever struck you how many of the plays of Euripides have a title beginning with 'i' or 'e' (or, what is much the same in Greek, 'hi' or 'he'): *Iphigeneia, Hippolytus, Electra, Helen, Hecuba* etc. …? It looks as if somehow, at some date, a single alphabetically arranged volume of the master's complete works managed to escape, when others were lost in fire, flood or whatever.

And just occasionally there is a dramatic find in the ancient papyri from the sands of Egypt. Most of the works of the Greek comic dramatist Menander reached us that way. So too (if you think that the monks maybe had it right in not bothering with Menander) did Aristotle's *Constitution of the Athenians* – actually probably the work of one of Aristotle's research assistants, but still a good find for anyone interested in Athenian history.

But what would I like to come up from any new excavation of the Villa of the Papyri at Herculaneum, where eighteenth-century diggers found loads of papyri rolls, the vast majority of which (apologies now to my philosophical colleagues) were rather dreary treatises from an also-ran Epicurean philosopher by the name of Philodemus?

I confess that I am not a tremendous enthusiast for more excavation on the Villa site. Various reasons. First, my feeling is that – if you have millions of euros to spend – you'd be better off preserving the parts of the ancient town of Herculaneum that have already been dug up, but are so badly crumbling that they won't make it to the next century. Second, I'm not honestly sure that we are desperate for much more classical literature, when we haven't really studied very hard vast tracts of what we already possess. Third, when most of what has come up from the Villa so far has been Philodemus, I don't see much reason to be optimistic about finding a more varied selection if we only dig deeper. (This place was obviously the bolt-hole of an obsessive Philodemus fan.)

But if I had to pick my 5 favourite lost classics to find in the lava, what would they be?

First off (and I'm scrupulously sticking to Latin – and written before the eruption of Vesuvius in 79 AD here) would be the *Autobiography of Agrippina*, Nero's mum.

We know she wrote one, and quite what she had to say about the death of her husband Claudius (those mushrooms?) would be fascinating to discover. Besides, we need some more women's literature from the ancient world.

Second, I'd have Ovid's play *Medea*. This is partly on the principle that you couldn't ever have enough of Ovid – than whom none was ever cleverer and funnier. And it would be good to see what he did with the story of a jealous child-murderer.

Third, I'd like the complete poetical works of Cicero. Poor old orator Cicero has had a really bad press for his poetry. Not helped by the 70 odd lines he himself quoted in one of his essays from his own epic poem *On His Own Consulship* (this included, as we know from other sources, the memorable bit of doggerel '*O fortunatam natam me consule Romam*' = 'Rome was born a lucky city,/when I as consul wrote this ditty', or sort of …). I'd like to see what it looked like when we saw the lot.

The **fourth** is going to play it safe. I'll take Ennius' *Annales* – his multi-volume epic on the history of Rome from the fall of Troy to the second century BC. Before Virgil, this was the national epic of Rome. And although some fragments survive, they're not really enough to see how the whole thing works.

Fifth, the wild card. The *Handbooks on Divination* by Umbricius Melior. Melior was the favourite *haruspex* (Etruscan diviner) of the short-lived emperor Galba (who followed Nero, 68/69 AD) and he's known to have written handbooks on his skill. This would be an insider's view on reading the omens in livers and the flights of bird … which might just help us see how this bit of ancient religion worked (there speaks the historian of religion!).

Does anyone have better ideas? And remember, not after 79 AD please.

Comments

Commenters did indeed have other ideas:

The rest of Cornelius Nepos

The emperor Claudius' Etruscan Histories
Calvus and Cinna the Poet
The first two books of Curtius Rufus
Suetonius' Lives of the Whores
Clodia's account of the liaison with Catullus
Varro's Three-headed Monster *(on the First Triumvirate)*
The rest of Sulpicia
The Amores *of Gallus*
The collected letters of Atticus …

But some had more to say:

A cute idea on the transmission of Euripides … Seeing as some of
the Euripides plays in your list begin with Eta and others Epsilon,
does this mean that a corollary of your hypothesis is that there
were no plays whose title began with Zeta or Theta? I'll let the
digs against Philodemus go for now … Great literature it might
not be, but I'm not sure Cicero's poetry would be a better bet. And
have you ever looked at Philodemus' poetry? You might like that.
JAMES

This correspondence recalls a conversation years ago at a
conference when folk started enumerating books written on
the principle of the solitary Highland lass's thoughts about
Wordsworth which they would like to read. Someone suggested,
'The Justice of Lloyd Jones by Zeus', someone else 'Syme, by
Tacitus'. 'What about Syme by the author of the *Historia Augusta*?'
asked a wit. 'They could not find anyone to sign the contract' came
the reply.

    [Untranslatable classical joke: ed.]
OLIVER NICHOLSON

Why didn't the Athenians give the women the vote?

8 November 2007

I have had a dreary cold, so I can't claim I was particularly looking forward to the three consecutive hours on the Critics (ancient and modern) of Athenian Democracy, but the students – pairs of my college first years – got me engaged. (If they didn't, this job would be a lot less worth doing.)

One of the issues we skirted round was, of course, the Woman Question. Why didn't those lovely democratic fifth-century Athenians give women political rights? And do we think worse of them for not doing so?

It's easy enough to toe the party line here. You can't apply modern criteria to ancient Athens. Within Athenian culture women were assumed to be unpolitical animals. Their job was to bear citizen children. They were, almost by definition, incapable of taking the responsible, informed decisions demanded of the (male) citizen body. Different from us, of course; but that's how the ancients, not just the Athenians, were.

So far, so good. But the problem is trying to imagine what it would actually be like to think of women in those terms. What would it feel like to feel that women were, by definition, excluded from political power, that it would be simply bonkers to include them (a question, needless to say, that applies to many cultures other than fifth-century Athens).

The analogy we tried was children. If someone were now to suggest that the under-tens should have the vote, we would bring out all those arguments that the Athenians would have brought out against women. They can't understand the decisions they would have to make. They still need the protection of their parents. It would be irresponsible to entrust major decisions of state or finance to them. In short, it would be bonkers.

Yet could we imagine a world in the far distant future where children had the vote? Could we imagine a world which derided our twenty-first-century 'folly' in depriving a clever nine-year-old of her citizenly rights, while driving the frail 95-year-old to the polling station to put her cross by whoever happened to take her fancy on the morning?

Maybe we almost could? And maybe in the process we were beginning to empathise a bit better with the assumptions of the Athenian misogynists – and so understand the ancient world in a different way. And maybe in the process we were beginning to understand something more about 'the invention of childhood', too.

And maybe my sore throat was receding in the fun of it all.

Want a motto? Do it in Latin.

26 November 2007

It is a truth universally acknowledged that a society in search of a slogan must be in need of Latin – which usually puts things snappier and shorter and cleverer than the poor old English vernacular. I mean, could you ever capture *'Per Ardua ad Astra'* quite so neatly in our mother tongue? 'Through struggles to the stars' seems horribly cumbersome. It's actually only one word more, it feels more like three times as long. I've seen some nice parodies, as it happens … *'Per ardua ad nauseam'* – or *'Per ardua ad Robin Reliant (can't afford an Astra)'*

I *know* this truth to be fairly universally acknowledged, as my Faculty in Cambridge gets so many requests from rugby clubs, charities, WIs, etc., to turn some reassuring platitude into a Latin slogan that we have a specially designated motto-writer. Professor X (I'm not going to reveal his name for fear of increasing the work load beyond what is manageable) is kept pretty busy.

The recent competition for devising a new British motto had Latin entries that fell into two camps: a few who picked up an existing Latin slogan and redeployed it more or less appropriately; and most, who tried their hand at their own bit of Latin. The results of this were what my older colleagues would call *'alpha/gamma'* – that is, occasionally brilliant but let down by some awful Latin grammar (or, alternatively, disappointing in their grip on the Latin language but enlivened by flashes of genius).

Playing safe with *bona fide* Latin was '*O tempora O mores*' ('What times, what customs!') This is a quote from Cicero in 63 BCE railing in the senate against the standards of his own day and at the terrorist Catiline, who was supposed to be bringing down civilisation as Cicero knew it and planning to nuke Rome. The only trouble is, it is just as likely that Catiline was a relatively innocent stooge, set up by Cicero looking for reds under the bed, and for an excuse for a brutal campaign of summary executions (or, in our nicer days, detention without trial) … not a dangerous 'terrorist' at all. So all the more appropriate, then?

The trouble with inventing your own Latin is quite how to make it sound clever rather than 'dog'. Not many succeeded. A few admitted their ignorance. One thought that 'National mottoes are for wimps' might sound better in Latin, but didn't risk it. Another asked for the Latin for 'Keep a stiff upper lip'.

What would that be?

Well, here we must go back to what our teachers taught us. The way you translate Latin is not 'word for word' – but going for the nugget of sense (that's why, they said, translating Churchill's speeches into Latin – a task on which I spent many days of my youth – was such a good training in understanding).

So, to take the earlier case, we won't be going for '*Tene labrum rigidum*' (literally 'Keep a stiff lip' – a phrase no Roman would have even begun to understand). But something more like '*Vincit qui se vincit*' ('He conquers who conquers himself' – the motto of self-control). It's a bit of a cheat actually, because the slogan was already a Latin one, included in an under-rated proverb collection of the first century BC.

As for the 'wimps', it would certainly involve the Latin *molles* ('softies'), but I'm not quite sure yet how I'd render 'national slogans'. Any ideas?

For the rest there was an awful lot of very funny 'dog' Latin (and don't forget that most 'dog' is actually meant to be funny). Sorry, it was a nice try with *'Perdisimus homines sumus'* – but some more mugging up is needed here on noun and adjective endings (*'Perdidissimi homines sumus'*, if you must – 'What wretches we are')! And much as I liked *'Magnus frater spectat te'* ('Big brother is watching you'), I would have to opt for *'Omnes videantur'* ('Let all be seen'). The same principles are at work here as with the Churchill: go for the nugget of sense, not for the words.

But what would I choose as my own motto? Well, I'm going back to real Latin and I've got a clear favourite: *'Capax imperii'* ('Capable of ruling').

That sounds grimly self-satisfied on its own, but you need to know what comes next. For those two words are part of what the historian Tacitus says, summing up the career of the elderly, few-month emperor Galba (68–9 AD). What follows is key. He had looked promising before he came to the throne, says Tacitus, but proved hopeless: he was *'capax imperii nisi imperasset'*. He was capable of ruling, if only he hadn't ruled. Or, as one smart translator put it, 'He had a great future behind him.'

That's Britain really: *capax imperii ... nisi ...* (and don't forget the *nisi*).

Labouring classicists – and New Year resolutions

1 January 2008

It's New Year's day and my birthday (OK ... 53). And my devotion to study on days that might in other circumstances be devoted to jollity is, I am afraid, getting to be a habit.

Today, I've been writing a paper for a big Classics conference in Chicago, where I'm going on Thursday. I promised a talk on 'working-class engagement in Classics' in the nineteenth century. I've been fed up for a long time with the usual line that Classics has always been an exclusively élite subject, designed only to shore up such dubious notions as British imperialism and the uncontestable superiority of the British élite.

The idea in proposing this paper was to try to get some flesh on those doubts. It turns out that I only have to talk for 20 minutes, into which you can hardly squeeze much of an argument. But even so I've left it a bit to the last minute. Hence full steam ahead today.

Actually – never mind the argument of the paper – I've found some tremendous characters. My particular favourite is Alfred Williams, born 1877, and author of *Life in a Railway Factory*, who taught himself Greek and Latin, partly by chalking up his irregular verbs on the casing of his forge.

Needless to say, this was a little trick which (however innocent) didn't appeal to the foreman. To stop Williams using the side of his forge as an *aide memoire* for the nastier parts of the '—*mi* verbs' (classicists will understand and sympathise), he had it covered with oil. Even this didn't stop Williams. As his first biographer explained, 'With characteristic determination Alf dared to clean off the oil thoroughly – in his own time of course, for he was always careful to avoid placing a weapon in the hand of his oppressor – and rewrote the Greek.'

There was a celebrity element in all this. The *Daily Mirror* in 1910 carried a picture of Alf composing a sonnet in his lunch break, in front of an audience which apparently included 'Mr Swinburne' (it can't have been the poet *Swinburne*, who died in 1909 – but it still makes me wonder how far the cultural establishment had taken over this autodidact).

A close second for me comes a woman poet, whom I should have known before – as she's a great symbol for all us female classicists. This is Ann Yearsley, a late eighteenth-century milkmaid, who penned a wonderful satire entitled *Addressed to Ignorance: occasioned by a Gentleman's desiring the Author never to assume a Knowledge of the Ancients*. In it, the great heroes of antiquity have been turned into animas or homely British labourers. ('Stout Ajax, the form of a butcher now takes …' and so on). Up yours is, I think, the message.

Comments

A great-uncle of mine, who would have been roughly contemporary with Alfred Williams, taught himself Latin and Greek while carting books to and fro in the behind-the-scenes recesses of the Bodleian for the learned men to read. But that's as much as I know and I had that from my mother, who has gone where no further enquiry is possible, so he's not a suitable candidate for inclusion in your paper.

DAVID KIRWAN

Obituaries of library staff in the Bodleian Library Record until recently sometimes recorded that the librarian (often a distinguished figure) had started life as a 'Bodley boy' – a young man (or woman) who had come to the Library on leaving school at 14 or so and after some years' work there was able to do an Oxford degree at the Library's expense. Did Cambridge have such a scheme?

OLIVER NICHOLSON

The rape of Britannia

30 January 2008

I shall be rather sad if Britannia does indeed, as the Prime
Minister plans, disappear from British coins. After all, it's
part of the point of a modern coin design that it should
include some hoary old symbol that is simultaneously easily
recognisable and also not fully comprehensible (or not
comprehensible without a bit of research, anyway).

One of the Greek euros has the Rape of Europa on it: a
frisky bull about to run off with – and worse – an innocent
young maid. (Imagine what the New Labour moral police
would have done with that one.) And what on earth was that
little bird on the old farthing? Was it a wren or a robin? And
why?

So Britannia fits the bill rather nicely. An appropriately
antique goddess, invented by the Romans, as a symbol of their
new province, and used on British coins since the seventeenth
century. If she goes, I don't hold out much hope, long term,
for that nice bit of Virgil ('*decus et tutamen*', '*an ornament and
a safeguard*' – from *Aeneid* Book V) around the pound coin. I
have a sneaking suspicion that Mr Brown isn't much of a fan of
Latin.

But while the traditionalists lament Britannia's
disappearance, they might like to reflect on her first
appearance in Roman art. As rape victim of the doddery old
emperor Claudius.

She is first used on a coin under the emperor Hadrian
in the second century AD, sitting on her usual rock. But her

premiere, so far as we know, was on a large building put up in
the town of Aphrodisias (in modern Turkey, not all that far
from Ephesus): the so-called 'Sebasteion', a building complex
of temple and porticoes, probably finished in the reign of the
emperor Nero, and dedicated to Aphrodite and the Roman
emperors/gods (the '*sebastoi*' in Greek).

It's loaded with sculpture (in fact, Aphrodisias, which is still
being excavated, is the place where some of the best ancient
sculpture has been discovered over the last few decades). There
are personifications of the tribes and peoples of the Roman
empire, scenes from myth (from Leda and the Swan to Orestes
at Delphi). And then there are more specifically Roman
images. One panel shows a heroically nude emperor Claudius
shaking hands with his wife (and murderess, if you believe the
stories), Agrippina. Another has Agrippina crowning her son
Nero with a laurel wreath.

Yet another is the Britannia panel. Claudius, naked again
apart from a bit of weaponry, is about to do something very
nasty to a sprawling Britannia, whom he's pulling back by
her flowing hair. She's dressed in a tunic already falling away

from her breasts, and some little barbarian boots. We know it's Claudius and Britannia because there's an inscription going with it that names them both.

As a commemoration of Claudius' conquest of Britain, it's about as classic a version of the erotics of military victory as you could wish for. And it goes with another panel from the monument, which is an even more titillating picture of Nero having his way with Armenia.

It's a useful antidote to the confident, bellicose Britannia ruling the waves on British coins. She who is victor was once victim; empires rise and fall; power comes and goes.

Of course, it's exactly these ambivalences and mixed messages that make such old classical symbols so good for the coinage. Pity we can't celebrate that, rather than just chuck them out.

Comments

I've sometimes wondered who proposed '*decus et tutamen*' for the pound coin. Was it some wit at the Bank of England with a good knowledge of the *Aeneid*? For the phrase refers to a breastplate that two attendants could hardly lift on their shoulders and carry away. Was the idea that this chunky new pound coin would weigh down your pocket or make your purse too heavy to carry?

MICHAEL BULLEY

The question of '*decus et tutamen*' on the pound coin is even more intriguing: the breastplate in question is awarded as *second* prize, and the narrator comments that the Trojan attendants can barely carry it between two of them – yet when it had belonged to the

Greek Demoleos, he could run about the battlefield at Troy in it. (*Aeneid* 5.258ff.)

So – is the message that history is too great a burden for Britain and we will always be inferior to the heroic past and the weight of Eastern and Mediterranean tradition we carry?

RICHARD

Surely '*decus et tutamen*' on the Thatcher (brassy and thinks it's a sovereign) was a motto used on coins at the time of the Restoration of Charles II (who also had Britannia modelled on one of his lady friends). God knows the meaning of the twiddles on the Blair (gilded on the edges, but base metal in the middle).

OLIVER NICHOLSON

Boudicca, Godiva, Matilda, Castlemaine, Emily Brontë, Eleanor Marx and Christine Keeler on future coins and notes, please!

XJY

It looks as if Britain could keep '*decus et tutamen*' if it wanted to, when it finally takes the plunge and adopts the euro. I've just spread my loose change in front of me and I see that, whereas the French 2 euro has no writing on the rim, the Netherlands one has. I also notice that, among these 30 or so coins, at least two nations are represented for each denomination. So that's another good thing about the euro: it puts internationalism into practice. I can go out tomorrow and buy things in the town with the solid metal currency of half a dozen countries all mixed together. *Pax Romana* the second!

MICHAEL BULLEY

What made the Romans laugh?

11 February 2008

This is my new project, which I'm soon going to be working on full time and full speed. But, as I was down to give a lecture to a group of 'lifelong learners' on Saturday night (they were spending their weekend reading Latin at the University's Continuing Education Centre at Madingley Hall), I decided to give them a first taster.

So we spent an hour looking at Roman jokes. It's a richer subject than you might imagine, though it's a shame that some of the best texts haven't survived. Just think what you could have done with the 150 volumes of joke anthologies by one Melissus, a contemporary of the emperor Augustus.

Still, I tried out some of those we do still have, curious to see how they went down.

The winner, I think, wasn't exactly a joke, but a bit of Roman imperial sit-com. It's a story about the bonkers emperor Elagabalus, recounted in the hugely unreliable late imperial series of biographies known as the *Historia Augusta*. It still had them laughing on Saturday:

> He had the custom of asking to dinner eight bald men, or else eight one-eyed men or eight men who suffered from gout, or eight deaf men, or eight men of dark complexion, or eight tall men or eight fat men – his purpose being in the case of these last, since they could not be accompanied on one couch, to call forth general laughter.

Elagabalus had a strong suit in practical jokes, and can be credited with the invention of a Roman version of the whoopee cushion. But they had a dangerous side, too. He was the emperor (again according to the *Historia Augusta*) who showered his guests with so many rose petals they suffocated and died.

But as for jokes proper, the winner was an ancient version of a 'nutty professor' joke.

The source for this is a curious compilation of about 250 jokes in Greek, probably put together in the fifth or sixth century AD, but including a good number of – even by then – very old chestnuts. It's called *'Philogelos'* in Greek, or 'Laughter Lover' (and there's a 1980s translation still available by Barry Baldwin).

The first hundred or so are all 'nutty professor' jokes (*scholastikos* in the Greek). Saturday's favourite was this one:

'That slave you sold me died,' a man complained to a nutty professor.

'Well, I swear by all the gods, he never did anything like that when I had him.'

Also raising quite a smile was one of the 'Abderite' jokes (that's, I'm afraid, the ancient equivalent of the Irishman or Belgian joke):

Seeing a eunuch chatting with a woman, an Abderite asked him if it was his wife.

The eunuch replied that people like him could not have wives.

'Ah then, she must be your daughter.'

And finally, in third place, was one of a category not so
familiar from our own repertoire – that is, jokes about blokes
with bad breath:

> A man with bad breath went to the doctor and said,
> 'Look, Doctor, my uvula is lower than it should be [a
> regular anxiety among the ancients, ed.].'
>   'Phew!' gasped the doctor, as the man opened his
> mouth to show him. 'It's not your uvula that has gone
> down, it's your arsehole that has come up.'

No, don't ask me to explain, if you didn't get it.

Comments

What makes people laugh is very culturally and no doubt
historically various. It is certainly not equivalent to finding
something funny. In central Africa, laughter expresses, or attempts
to conceal embarrassment. For example, in a traffic accident,
the culprit may well laugh and the foreign victim is liable to
misinterpret this as not caring, or even as an added insult …
   I was once at a performance of *Romeo and Juliet* in Lesotho.
At the suicide of Romeo, the junior Basotho audience laughed
uproariously, much to the obvious demoralisation of the British
performers.
PAUL POTTS

Eight fat men on a sofa: accompanied by whom?
   I think people in Lesotho are not the only ones who laugh to
conceal their embarrassment.
ANTHONY ALCOCK

Did St Valentine Exist?

13 February 2008

Valentine's Day comes with a sense of relief for the middle-aged. At least you are not on tenterhooks about what might, or might not, come in the mail. Truth to tell, apart from welcome tokens of affection from the husband, I don't think I have ever received a Valentine – of the traditional, unexpected, 'wonder who it is' sort.

Nor for that matter have I ever sent one, so far as I can remember. Except years ago as a joke to a senior colleague, who was instantly convinced that it was from someone else. The less said about this the better.

None of which stops me being curious about the Roman history of all this. In fact, for all of you wondering if there was ever a real Saint Valentinus, the good news is that there was not just one, but three.

The bad news is that we know almost nothing reliable about him/them. Earnest and detailed articles about his true history have, I am afraid, fallen for some very unreliable parts of Valentine's myth.

The 'facts' are these.

There are three possible Valentines for our purposes (leaving out the tens of other saints also known by that name – a common one in the Roman empire):

A stray North African
A bishop of Terni (in Italy)
A priest in Rome

So far Wiki is reliable, but then – though it's actually better than most accounts – it gets a bit dodgier.

The stray North African doesn't actually get you very far. The second two were both supposed to have been martyred on 14 February, though not necessarily in the same year, and may indeed have been the same person (if they ever existed, that is).

We don't have any contemporary accounts of the martyrdom of this pair (?one). But there is a sixth- or seventh-century version which gives them their separate stories. Here the Roman Valentine is said to have been martyred under the emperor Claudius – Claudius Gothicus (268–70). Only trouble is that Claudius Gothicus was a tolerator of Christians, and was hardly in Rome to persecute Christians anyway. The other Valentine, of Terni, may have been martyred in the 270s (no firm date is given), but his story and miracles are not unlike his Roman namesake – more reason for wondering if they are the same. No sign, in either case, of being a patron saint of lovers.

According to the most rigorous modern scholar of our saint (Jack B. Oruch, who wrote a famous article on the subject in *Speculum* for 1981), that particular element was not actually invented until Chaucer – who was looking for a lovers' saint to mark the start of spring. (February, start of spring before global warming? Well, it was helped, apparently, by the calendar being out of synch with the seasons in the fourteenth century.)

But there is another ingenious twist, which appeals to me – although it is, almost certainly, quite wrong. One smart scholar of the eighteenth century shrewdly asked what the pagan Romans would have been doing on 14 February. Answer: in Rome itself, they were in the middle of the weird festival of the Lupercalia (in which naked young men raced round the city, beating with thongs any woman lucky enough to get in their way). One thing we know is that in the late fifth century AD Pope Gelasius was angry to find his flock still enjoying this pagan festival, when they should have been being good Christians. So what does he do? He invents St Valentine's day, to give his wayward people a fun, but Christian, festival to replace the Lupercalia.

Lovely idea, but not a shred of evidence.

Comments

I'm not sure which of the many Valentines it is, but what are claimed to be the bones of St Valentine are at present in the Carmelite church in Whitefriars Street, Dublin. An Irish Carmelite preacher so impressed Pope Gregory XVI by his preaching when he visited Rome in 1836 that he was given a casket containing the saint's bones when he left to return to Ireland. Accompanying them was a papal certificate of authenticity. However, in the current Roman calendar February 14th is the feast of Sts Cyril and Methodius, apostles to the Slavs and supposed originators of the Cyrillic alphabet. Perhaps St Valentine has been silently disavowed.

DAVID KIRWAN

I would like to think that Valentine was the gnostic thinker of the 2nd cent. AD responsible for the Sophia myth recounted in a couple of Nag Hammadi texts. Sophia, an outer aeon, 'fell' and was responsible for the creation of the material (*hylic*) world, but was ultimately restored to her former status by her *syzygy*, Christ, who gave the *hylic* world a fighting chance of survival. Basically, a boy meets girl story.

ANTHONY ALCOCK

I am shocked on reading David Kirwan's post that the Roman calendar still has a feast of St Cyril. Wasn't he the bishop of Alexandria who had Hypatia murdered so tragically?

ARINDAM BANDYOPADHAYA

Cyril seems to have been a fairly unscrupulous ecclesiastical politician, who was very probably deeply engaged in a power struggle with the Prefect of the city, Orestes. Hypatia, who seems to have been friendly with Orestes, may have got in the way. Kingsley's account may not be so far from the truth, assuming of course that there is such a thing. Socrates, in his *Church History*, accuses Cyril of plundering the Novatian churches and expelling the Jews from Alexandria. Cyril certainly seems to have had a fairly shrewd idea of how to control the hairy hooligans who inhabited the desert in various parts of Egypt.

ANTHONY ALCOCK

A day in Guantanamo

21 February 2008

OK, not quite. But I have just spent a day in an orange Guantanamo style jumpsuit, as part of our student Amnesty Group's 'Orange Wednesday'. This was a bit of harmless and colourful street theatre, designed to draw attention to the injustices of illegal detention all over the world. A few hundred of us, mostly students but some staff, went about our daily business dressed as Guantanamo detainees.

I volunteered for this fancy dress partly because I believe in the cause. But partly because most students seem so unbothered by issues of surveillance, civil liberties and human rights that it is important to show some solidarity with those who are.

That said, I'm afraid I've lost some of my old knack for political action.

The first problem was: was I going to be able to get into the damn suit? (Not an issue for the poor thin creatures at the real Guantanamo, needless to say.) I had ordered an extra-large, but still had my doubts – particularly when the word went about that they only came in one size.

The good news was that it fitted. The bad news was that once in, it was almost impossible to get out. Going to the loo involved a good five minutes' twisting and wriggling, before I could manage to release my shoulders and gradually pull the whole thing down.

No coffee for the day seemed the obvious answer to that one. But worse was the fact that, even when strutting about the Faculty Library in my bright orange, I still didn't seem to manage to get the Guantanamo message across.

Maybe classicists really are the absent-minded, faraway creatures that I'm always claiming they're not. Or maybe, as one of my colleagues suggested, the handbag I was carrying slightly detracted from the overall impact. But the commonest reaction I got, if anything, was, 'Gosh, you're bright today', 'Wow, great colour', etc.

One wag asked me if I'd just been hired by Drainco. (Their guys do look pretty similar, but I thought actually I looked closer to an Easyjet engineer.) Another, who at least got the point, asked if I was dressed up to celebrate Fidel Castro's departure.

I rather envied one of my classicist co-demonstrators who had been giving a lecture and so at least was able to explain to his captive audience why he was so colourfully dressed (and that he wasn't actually moonlighting as the drain unblocker).

Was it this difficult in the 70s? I don't remember it being so. But perhaps in truth it was.

Comments

I am continually amazed at the ignorance of the politically active. In fact, orange jumpsuits are a virtual uniform for ALL prisoners in the US. Ordinary offenders appear in court wearing them regularly, not least on TV. And they are also shackled while being led into court, though not in the Box. Similarly, in the comics of my childhood (which you *TLS* types are now trying to make me call 'graphic novels'), convicts were always pictured in black and white stripes. And of course with ball and chain. Guantanamo is a bad place, and we would be glad to see it closed, but the prisoners were apprehended in circumstances which would lead rational people to suspect they may be bad lots.

WAVYDAVY

Prince Harry: the Roman solution

3 March 2008

I've found the adulation of Prince Harry – who appears to have spent a couple of months driving a laptop and something called a 'Spartan vehicle' in Afghanistan – a bit hard to take. OK, it's easy for me to sneer, as I haven't been in the Taliban firing line, but you know what I mean. Wouldn't it actually have been more honourable if he had faced danger on some humanitarian project rather than pushing forward whatever military folly we're committing in Afghanistan?

Almost equally insufferable were the interviews with the said youth, including his memorable comment about how he didn't like England much. To this, I had two reactions. One is that it is Harry's *job* to like England. The rest of us are allowed to feel as ambivalent as we like. But, as third in line to the throne, he doesn't have that luxury (though he has plenty of other ones). So he'd better just get on with it.

Second is that, if it's the paparazzi who are bothering him, then maybe fewer late night romps at Boujis nightclub could do the trick.

But further thought suggested that there was a Roman angle to this trip of the young prince to the military front line. In fact, Roman emperors knew a thing or two about the problems of sending the son and heir off to war.

The emperor Augustus had particularly bad luck. Two of his grandchildren and chosen heirs were sent to the front and never came back. Young Lucius was off to fight in Spain, but died at Marseilles on the way out. That was in 2 AD. In 4 AD, his brother Gaius died in the east, after a war wound.

At least we've got Harry back.

Tiberius had bad luck of the opposite kind. He sent his adopted son Germanicus to the German frontier. The glamorous prince didn't manage to round up Arminius, the chief terrorist of the region – who was presumably holed up, Osama-like, in a cave somewhere. But he did score a number of successes which went down rather too well in Rome for the peace of mind of his jealous father.

Tiberius' answer was to declare the war resoundingly finished (even though it wasn't) and bring him back home for a triumph in 17 AD. It must have been uncomfortable for the emperor, putting on a grateful face at the ceremony. But at least it had put a stop to his victories.

Not that it was more than a temporary solution. Germanicus went off to the eastern frontier in 18 AD. The next year he died in suspicious circumstances in Antioch. The Roman governor of Syria was tried for his murder. Gossip on the street was that he had been poisoned at Tiberius' orders.

Whatever the awkwardness of Harry's current position, this story reminds us that his seniors must be grateful that he didn't pull off any really major heroics. Imagine that, armed only with his laptop and Spartan vehicle, he had single-handedly rescued 20 wounded men under Taliban fire. The tabloids would have loved it. But the political problems of what to do with him next would have been a lot worse.

And who would have played Tiberius?

Comments

This one prompted a lot of comments on the same lines ('Beard is disgusting … Hats off to Harry', 'Get back to reading your dusty books on Roman history', 'Why don't you make yourself useful and go and knit something', 'Leave Harry alone!!!', 'Stick to making jam Mary', 'What is this Beard woman wittering on about?'), but a few took a different, or more reflective, line:

Come on, Mary, be fair. Prince Harry is a young army officer who is obviously perfectly all right and, I suspect, good at his job when he is given something to do – and lets off steam rather too publicly when idle. In my view we have here a prime example of the modern hysterical, celebrity-orientated media in full cry.

You may think, as I do, that the fourth (British) Afghan War is a completely unnecessary and all round disastrous affair with no apparent purpose, as opposed to cooked up excuses, but it does not alter the fact that our troops have been sent there to fight and are doing so with considerable tactical success. The fact that strategically it can make little difference is not their fault but that of our abysmal politicians.

RICHARD H

So, according to Professor Beard:

1 Harry should not fight for his country.
2 He should be more patriotic.
3 He should not enjoy his life while here.

I remember studying at Cambridge. This brings it back.

TOM

Well played, Mary. Almost as much bile generated by this piece as by the one featuring Parthenon.

ANTHONY ALCOCK

'do some knitting'… 'make some jam'…

I don't feel that those who respond this way to what they see as Beard's Nonsense make themselves seem very thoughtful commentators. (I seem to remember that there were rumours, when men waved banners saying 'iron my shirt' at a Hillary Clinton rally, that the Clinton camp had arranged for this to happen, since they in fact made Clinton look good, in that people are more attractive when their enemies are clearly idiots.)

Prof. Beard: I don't think you should retire from the world of public comment for a good long time. But if at some time in the future you were to turn (NB 'remote future conditional') into a Clapped Out Academic with Nothing Left to Say, I suggest you don't bother with jam or knitting (unless you really want to) and settle instead for the traditional and gender-neutral combination of food, novels and gentle alcoholism.

So next time somebody wants to tell the Prof. to shut up, may I suggest a non-sexist cry of 'Beard, go and have a drink'?

RICHARD

Who says knitting and Classics are incompatible. I always knit my way through department meetings and two of my colleagues have now joined me – a lifted knitting needle is an excellent way of intervening on a point of order.

I am afraid I do not understand how the bravery of Prince Harry is meant to parallel the career of Germanicus. But I do know that what he has done requires courage I cannot even conceive of. And not the least impressive thing about him has been the

fact that he and his father on his return both made the point
(resolutely under-reported by the press) that if he was a hero so
equally were the other 8000 folk serving Queen and country in
the east.

OLIVER NICHOLSON

Dead men's books

12 March 2008

When my mother was dying, she made it very clear that she didn't want anyone wearing her clothes after she was dead. I didn't quite understand this at the time. After all, she would happily have given away her internal organs if they hadn't been past their sell-by date. And she happily distributed her used clothes during her lifetime. So why not after her death?

I vaguely supposed that it was something to do with the final annihilation that people going through, choosing or rejecting your clothes would seem to entail. And didn't give it much more thought.

But last week I came face to face with that sense of annihilation when the vultures (self included) descended to take the pickings of my old, recently dead, supervisor's books.

For many academics, books have much the same significance as clothes. They are what you use every day and you have your favourites as well as your expensive mistakes. Not to mention the carefully mended, the carelessly torn, the messily annotated.

The trouble is what happens to them when you've gone to the great library in the sky.

In Cambridge, the labour of disposal often falls to your college – which normally takes its pick for the college library, then lets the local second-hand bookseller take his pick and make a tidy profit.

John Crook's college had made a different decision. They announced an afternoon when college and faculty, students and staff, would be let into his old rooms to buy any book they wanted for a pound, though larger donations were welcome. All profits were to go to a fund for the college staff. It was a nice idea – designed, I guess, to ensure that the old man's books went to those who would use and value them.

In fact it turned into a truly ghastly occasion.

The omens were bad when I walked into the college and met one of my graduate students who said that he'd just bought a copy of my PhD thesis. Now, it couldn't have gone to a better home, and I'm truly glad he got it. But I still felt that somehow it was a personal thing between me and Crook – not something to be flogged for a quid.

It was altogether worse when I got in his rooms. They were emptier than he had left them, but his cap was still there, the desk in the same place and all the books still on the shelves – or some of them were. For the vultures were already at work, rifling through them section by section, picking out some, casually rejecting others. A few people had piles numbering what looked like hundreds of volumes.

Couldn't they have put the books on tables? Or just somewhere else? It seemed like theft taking them from the shelves where some of them have spent the last 50 years.

The worst moment was when I heard one student bibliophile loudly bark: 'Is it a presentation copy?' I could have thumped the boy. I wanted to say, 'That book was given to him by a friend, who wrote in it for him … and he then used it. It isn't a commodity which will enhance your collection because it's got an author's signature in it.' But what was the point? We were all there sniffing out the bargains, a bit like the first day of the sales.

Mum was right about her clothes, I thought.

Do physicists need French?

17 March 2008

If you have academically élite universities, it's only predictable
– indeed it's right and proper – that people debate exactly what
qualifications students should have to get into them.

A hundred years ago, the headlines were all about whether
ancient Greek should be a necessary qualification to get
into Cambridge. Technically speaking it wasn't actually a
qualification you needed to be admitted in the first place. But,
if you wanted an honours degree, you had to do a preliminary
exam in Greek soon after you arrived – which was pretty much
the same thing in practice.

The arguments went as you might expect. The abolitionists
claimed that the Greek requirement was preventing highly
intelligent boys (*sic*) from coming to Cambridge, if they
weren't already at a select group of socially élite schools (the
access argument). They also suggested that it was pretty
antediluvian requiring a dead language when you could
be getting the boys to learn a modern language, French or
German (the utility argument).

On the other side, the retentionists argued that Greek
was an essential part of a liberal education, and that it would
disappear from schools unless Cambridge continued to require
it. To this the abolitionists retorted that it wasn't Cambridge's
job to take responsibility for the school curriculum.

The arguments went on from 1870 to 1919, when in
the brave new post-war world the Greek requirement was

abolished (and, true to the retentionists' fears, the decline of Greek in schools had begun).

A hundred years on and the radical choice of the early twentieth century – namely French and German – are now in their turn to be toppled. Cambridge is planning no longer to require a modern language from all students across the board.

The arguments are strikingly reminiscent of those on 'The Greek Question', and both sides have a point.

On the one hand is the access argument. If only 17% of state schools now require pupils to study a foreign language after the age of 14, then you're *de facto* excluding a lot of potential students if you make it a necessary condition for Cambridge entrance. (Or, to put it another way, you'll find it hard to make your government access targets ...)

This is backed up by the utility argument. Why should we care if physicists know French, since the language of science is universal English?

On the other side is the argument that an élite university cannot be a monoglot university, and it is to challenge the very excellence of Cambridge as an institution to suggest that it should be producing graduates who know no language but their own. (That has been part of UCL's argument for introducing the requirement that Cambridge now plans to abolish.) And you can add to that the likely prediction that Cambridge's decision on this will further weaken the precarious position of modern languages in schools.

In my position, the safest place to be is on the fence. But deep down, as you've probably guessed, I am sure that this proposal cannot be right. It is the duty of a university such as Cambridge to stand up for the highest academic standards (that's a responsibility that being a world-class institution brings). If it believes that modern languages are an essential part of excellence, then it should be doing everything it can to ensure that all children have access to them (access in the real sense) – not acceding to short-term quick fixes to meet some cynical government target.

As for the argument that physicists don't need French … It may be that the international language of science is English, but do we really think that we are properly equipping our best scientists to work in the international world of Europe, China, India, etc., if they don't even know what it is *like* to learn a language to a decent level of competence? Isn't 'networking' something we are now supposed to train them to do? I bet that doesn't all happen in English.

Maybe the idea is that we are going to teach them all a foreign language when they get here. But I doubt it somehow.

Comments

Pour qu'elles comprennent mieux la culture contemporaine, il faudrait plutôt apprendre aux étudiantes de français les éléments de la physique …
TIM SLUCKIN

Tim: *Aux étudiantes seulement, ou aussi aux étudiants?*
SW FOSKA

Let's Get Rid of the Fascist Olympic Torch

26 March 2008

I don't quite understand how we have forgotten that the 'Olympic Torch' ceremony was invented by Hitler and his chums.

If ever there was an 'invented tradition' well worth stamping out, it is this ridiculous, fascist-inspired waste of money – which sends a Bunsen burner around the world at tremendous cost for several months before the Games, manned (and womanned) by people dressed up in pseudo-ancient Greek costume, no doubt feeling very silly.

In London, we are now told, it will soon be doing a mini tour, carried by a London bus, Docklands Light Railway and Dame Kelly Holmes (*inter alios*).

I can't quite work out whether most of the press reports are pleased at the pro-Tibetan protests which dented the hi-tech-assisted, sunbeam lighting ceremonial (plucky little Tibet poking the Chinese dragon where it, for once, might hurt); or whether they are a touch censorious at this upsetting of the peaceful, non-political programme of the Olympic Games that we have inherited from the ancient Greeks; or whether they are wondering what might happen to the UK in the ceremonies to come in 2012 (don't forget Iraq, Mr Blair/Brown …)

Hardly any commentator stops to mention that this silly torch ceremony has nothing to do with the ancient Greeks, and was really invented to be a magnificent shot in Leni

Riefenstahl's movie *Olympia* (choreographed by Carl Diem). This is one of Hitler's most pervasive legacies.

They also don't stop to mention that the ancient Olympics – far from being that sweet haven of peace – were pretty political anyway. Even in their heyday, they were often interrupted by the rough hand of Politics.

The classic case is the eligibility of Alexander the Great's ancestor, Alexander I of Macedon. When he turned up to compete in the early fifth century BC, the other Greeks said that he was a foreigner and so wasn't eligible. Eventually the gatekeepers allowed him to take part, but – although he finished first (equal) – he didn't get his name written into the official list of winners. (Hence, he is an awkward example on both sides for the modern argument about whether 'Macedonia' is 'Greek'. Does Alexander I prove the Greekness of the Macedonians, or *vice versa*?)

But there were plenty more political controversies. The worst was in 364 BC when the Games happened while Olympia was under enemy occupation, or more accurately in the middle of a war zone. In fact, the Arcadians (Olympia's neighbours in the Peloponnese) invaded during the pentathlon event and some of their soldiers looted the sacred treasures. So much for the 'Sacred Truce'.

That was only the tip of the iceberg. In the 380s Lysias, the Athenian orator and democratic hero, harangued his fellow countrymen, urging them more or less to wreck the Olympic village. Four and a half centuries later, the Olympic officials appear to have turned a blind eye and let the emperor Nero win whatever competition he wanted – in return for some rather generous investment at the Olympic site.

We may not like the politicisation of the Olympic Games, but let's not pretend that this is a modern invention.

Comments

Can't we just get rid of the modern Olympics altogether, and replace them with the Nemean Games?

DOROTHY KING

Feminism now: should boys play harps?

17 April 2008

Last week the main BBC news (plus the *Today* programme) was full of a piece of research which demonstrated a gender bias in choice of musical instruments. Whereas 90% of young harpists are (apparently) female, almost 80% of young tuba players are (apparently) male – and even more electric guitarists. Indeed, kids are encouraged in those choices by friends, teachers, society … you name it.

While parts of the planet were in meltdown, while Zimbabwe tottered, Kenya simmered and too few people were killed in Iraq to be newsworthy …THIS was transmitted as a piece of gender discrimination akin to the revelation (the sort of news we faced when I was a kid) that more girls than boys were encouraged to become nurses than doctors and *vice versa*.

After a short time, feeling a bit bad about this, as I was obviously supposed to, I found myself reflecting … do I care really if tuba players are largely male?

OK, I've seen *Billy Elliot*, and I know that it is rotten to be looked on as a wimp if you're a boy and you want to do ballet. I also know (from even more personal experience) that it can be rotten to be a girl and want to do blokeish things.

But this didn't seem to me to have much to do with the old doctors and nurses argument. The point about that was that girls chose to be nurses and got lower pay, less prestige and a lifetime of emptying bed-pans; boys chose to be doctors and got more money, more prestige, while prancing round in a white coat/suit and marrying a nurse. The gender choices cashed out into economic and status disadvantage.

But is that the same with musical instruments? Is there a built in advantage in learning the harp over the tuba, or *vice versa*? If not, shouldn't we just let the kids be gendered and just be pleased that they are learning any musical instrument at all? If it takes a tuba or a Fender to get boys interested in learning an instrument, well, phew … And if girls are inspired to go on with the cello by the sight of those old (and, of course, now sad) images of Jacqueline du Pré making love to her instrument, it's a small price to pay.

I thought it might have been more interesting if the survey (and no, I haven't read the original) had taken that other *Billy Elliot* theme and looked at class. How many working-class kids now learn to play any instrument at all?

Isn't that more of a worry?

Comments

It's wonky in a different way at the top, anyway – orchestras are full of men, on any/every instrument. I don't really think it matters much, so long as *everyone* is given a chance at possibly becoming a good musician.

The real gender problem in music is with the conductors … where are all the women?

NEWN1

I'm a woman and a musician – and I play what men still see as a 'male' instrument (the bass). I've been playing professionally for 20 years and, while meeting prejudice isn't now a 100 per cent experience, it can still be a weekly one. It can be tiresome and upsetting, impacting not only on my income, but on creative opportunities. At times, I have considered giving up music because of it, but being brought up in feminism's halcyon days when trying to become what I wanted to be as a woman was nearly as much a duty as a right, I have always dragged myself from my bed the next day to … Face the music. Besides, playing the bass is what I do.

I would say to Mary: Don't swap concern for one prejudice for a pet or preferred one. They are all important. Of course there is no contest between people starving in Zimbabwe or the mass rape and murder happening in the Congo, but thinking that sexism in British schools isn't important means we cannot demonstrate beautiful, healthy equality to the rest of the world either.

KLIMT

Dr Bowdler was ahead of us all.

Othello famously raged against the supposed infidelity of Desdemona:

'and shall she play the strumpet in my bed?'

The good doctor preserved the metre while making the line appropriate for family reading simply by deleting the initial 's' from the sixth word.

OLIVER NICHOLSON

Personally, I would far rather hear any half-decent ensemble composed of males and/or females on instruments they can actually play than be subjected to any more videos of vacuous sex objects flashing their flesh and surviving only due to the sophistication of studio electronics.

STEVE KIMBERLEY

Keep Lesbos for the Lesbians

5 May 2008

A tricky issue has just hit the Greek courts. Some residents of the island of Lesbos have just decided to resort to the law to prevent the 'Homosexual and Lesbian Community of Greece' from using the word Lesbian in its title.

The idea is that the heterosexual female denizens of the island don't much like the idea that when they claim they are Lesbian everyone assumes that they are gay. (It's a claim that might be stronger, I think, if the appellants in this case were women, not men representing their sisters ...) But if they are successful in their suit against the Greek organisation, the plan is to try to outlaw 'Lesbians' (as a word) worldwide.

The problem here is the sixth-century BC Greek poetess Sappho: born and bred in Lesbos, she addressed some of the most passionate erotic poetry the world has known to fellow women. An achievement which in the ancient world earned her the title '10th Muse'. Almost ever since Lesbos has been synonymous with lesbianism (in fact since the eighteenth century in British English).

This idea of decoupling Sappho, female homoeroticism and the island of Lesbos seems to me about as mad as trying to white out William Shakespeare from Stratford-upon-Avon.

In fact, Sappho is the sexiest thing to have come from the island in 3,000 years. Why on earth jack in the commercial possibilities?

The competition for most famous islander is not great. Alcaeus was also a Lesbian, another early poet, who famously claimed to throw away his shield on the battlefield and walk (?run) away – so giving rise to a whole tradition of ancient poetic military refuseniks.

You might also think of Theophrastus, fourth/third-century BC scientist, who wrote a wonderful analysis of different character types called *The Characters*.

In the modern world you might go for the poet Odysseas Elytis who won the Nobel Prize for Literature in 1979. But that's not quite the 10th Muse and, though his family came from Lesbos, he was actually born in Crete anyway.

So why on earth aren't the Lesbians (islanders, that is) *celebrating* Sappho and doing all they can to resurrect her poetry? Out of 9 volumes, only a handful of stuff survives. But more may be found. Only a few years ago another poem was discovered on an Egyptian papyrus. A nice middle-aged lyric about not having the knees to dance any more.

Why don't the islanders buy into this, instead of complaining about the supposed sexual 'insult'?

Comments

Why does your list of eminent Lesbians vault lightly (but in a manner not uncharacteristic of classical scholars) over roughly two thousand years of post-classical history. How about Zacharias of Mytilene, whose not unentertaining early Byzantine chronicle survives in a Syriac version – there is certainly more of him than there is of Sappho.

I find that *OED* gives no instance of Lesbian or lesbianism in its modern English sense earlier than 1870. It was possible for a respectable family in Willesden as late as 1898 (presumably admirers of Catullus, 'tenderest of Roman poets') to name their daughter Lesbia; she grew up to be Lesbia Scott, wife of a vicar of Chagford and author of an All Saints Day hymn of great charm, 'I Sing a Song of the Saints of God', more sung in the United States than in her native land. No doubt Alma-Tadema has much to answer for.

OLIVER NICHOLSON

The Lesbians also have ouzo, which is more palatable than poetry, for some. So, maybe they drink too much, that would explain this bizarre initiative.

GILLES

I don't see the problem. There are lesbians who aren't Lesbians, Lesbians who aren't lesbians and Lesbians who are lesbians, which is the same thing as lesbians who are Lesbians. What could be simpler?

MICHAEL BULLEY

Nicholson may be a whizz at looking things up in the *OED* but had he clicked on the link in note 3 of the Wikipedia article 'Lesbian' he would have found an interesting discussion and a reference to a book (Emma Donoghue, *Passions between Women: British Lesbian Culture 1668–1801*, London, 1993) which, it is claimed, establishes 'beyond doubt' 'that throughout the seventeenth and eighteenth centuries the word "Lesbian" was used in the very same sense as today'.

However, the term's relation to its geographical referent is worth considering. 'Lesbian' bears some superficial analogy to 'Sodomite', denoting someone who does what people in a certain place are reputed to do. But it was rarely alleged that all Lesbians did lesbian things (some of them were men, for a start). The term doubtless gained currency as a periphrasis or euphemism for 'Sapphist', initially more popular in English. (Rather like saying 'The Stagyrite' for 'Aristotle').

SWF nevertheless feels some sympathy with the Lesbiot cause, as the sexual meaning is an exogenous imposition from a more powerful culture and developed not only through the attribution of the practices of a single group member to the whole, but also in the more general context of attributing perversion to the Oriental other. (A comparable term is 'bugger', originally attributed to Bulgars, the alleged ethnic origin of religiously heterodox Cathars in southern France in the Middle Ages. But this last etymology is now only semantically vestigial so no ethnic offence is given or taken by the use of the term.)

SW FOSKA

I'm not sure about this. If 'Brit' were to become synonymous with 'sado-masochistic state terrorist', as well it might, I, as a Brit, might well be reluctant to allow myself to be identified as such.

PAUL POTTS

It's the people of Kos I feel for. Constantly accused of being lettuces. I wouldn't like anybody to call *my* sister a lettuce.

I can't say I find 'a nice middle-aged lyric about not having the knees to dance any more' a very enticing description of the new Sappho: trust me, folks, the arthritic ode is more exciting than this makes it sound …

Anyway, one of the ancient stories about Sappho's life (the ancients told lots of anecdotes of dubious or non-existent historicity about Sappho) had her married to a man called Kerkylas of Andros. Kerkus was a word for penis, and the name of the island Andros sounds the same as the genitive of the word for 'man'. One scholar suggested the translation 'Dick Allcock of the Isle of Man'. So it looks as if this story expresses the idea 'we all know what these Lesbians really want to put them right …'

RICHARD

In the nineteenth century, wasn't all homosexuality (and especially the male kind) referred to as 'Greek love' anyway?

It is presumably by some accident of linguistic development that 'Lesbian' became widely adopted, but 'Greek' fell by the wayside in favour of 'gay'. It could easily have been otherwise. We could be speaking today about 'Greek rights' or 'Greek pride' or 'Greek and Lesbian film festivals'. In which case, the Greeks generally would know how some of these Lesbians are apparently feeling …

HERESIARCH

The face of Julius Caesar? Come off it!

14 May 2008

What do you do if you are an archaeologist and you find a nice Roman portrait bust in the bottom of a river?

The answer is simple. You go through every book of Roman portraits and coins until you find some famous figure in Roman history who looks vaguely likely your man. It is laborious and time-consuming. But the principles are simple – it's like a game of snap.

Why bother? Because almost every newspaper in the Western world will be interested in your find if you say confidently that it is Cleopatra or Nero or Julius Caesar (and

even more interested if you say that this is the earliest statue
or the only one really taken from life – which is also a useful
cover-up for the fact that your statue doesn't look quite like all
the others supposed to represent the famous figure).

However beautiful or important your find, no newspaper
will be searching you out if you have only found Marcus
Cornelius Nonentito.

There's a long tradition to this game. Heinrich Schliemann
tried to convince the world that he had gazed upon the face
of Agamemnon. Almost every local archaeological society in
England was certain that the tiny little Roman villa they were
digging up was actually the governor's residence – and they
labelled the plans accordingly, 'Governor's wife's bedroom' and
so on.

Now we have the story of the only surviving statue of Julius
Caesar to be sculpted from life dragged out of the river at
Arles. Right?

This sculpture is, I should say, a very nice piece of work
– and looks remarkably good for something that has been at
the bottom of the Rhône for a couple of thousand years. There
is, I suppose, a remote possibility that it does represent Julius
Caesar, but no particular reason at all to think that it does –
still less to think that it was done from life.

The game of art-historical snap is a risky business, and
honestly you could find hundreds of Romans who, with the eye
of faith, look pretty much like this. Besides – despite all you
get told about the style of the portrait pinning it down to a few
years – this style of portraiture lasted for centuries at Rome.
There is nothing at all to suggest that it came from 49–46 BC.

The desperate archaeologist in this case has, of course,
found a nice reason for imagining how a made-from-life
portrait of Julius Caesar might have ended up at the bottom

of the Rhône. It was chucked there after Caesar had been assassinated and so had fallen from favour.

Has he forgotten that that was the very moment when Caesar was turned into a god?

Well, he might respond, the burghers of southern France took a dim view of such flummery. OK, so why did they throw that nice statue of Neptune, apparently found in the same haul, into the river too?

I'm afraid it's 'start again' time on the explanations for this one.

Comments

Plenty more suggestions for the identification of the mystery man were made by commentators. There were votes for, amongst others: Mel Gibson, Augustus, Mark Antony, Sid James, Tiberius Claudius Nero, George Bush, Claudius … and some longer comments.

How do we even know that it wasn't thrown into the river 'yesterday'? The handling of the nasal-labial folds doesn't look very Roman to me.

EILEEN

As you say, it's not a new phenomenon and I can't help thinking 'I have gazed upon the face of Agamemnon' was a rather good line. Back in the 18th century, Alexander Pope, in his 'Epistle to Dr Arbuthnot' was satirising wealthy collectors typified by Bufo, in whose library 'a true Pindar stood without a head'.

KATH

It's the closeness and beadiness of his eyes that make him resemble George Bush, features he shares with the Tivoli General. I disagree with the suggestion that it was meant for insertion into a statue-body. There is too much shoulder and chest for that. Insertable heads have only a neck.

What exactly is the problem with the handling of the naso-labial lines? They look to me like many other republican examples. Perhaps their doubling here is unusual, but an unusual stylistic feature is, as we all know, not a reason to assume a forgery.

LIZ MARLOWE

I think that what can happen with these '*plus éminents spécialistes*' is that Prof. X has a theory, as it might be the identification of the subject of a portrait, and bounces up to another professor, full of excitement, and runs it past him. If Prof. Y believes that it is complete hogwash he will say, 'Well, of course you might be right, but I wouldn't like to bet on it; have you considered factors a, b and c?' If, as might be the case here, Prof. Y believes that the theory is dubious, while not complete hogwash, he will probably say, 'What a brilliant idea! Quite probably you are right, though I suppose that a sceptic might want to be convinced on point a', or something like that.

Why? Well, Prof. X is full of the joys of spring and the exhilaration of discovery, and Prof. Y doesn't want to rain on his parade. And he knows that he hasn't spent as much time thinking about it as Prof. X has, and is likely to be disinclined to disagree with somebody who has done the donkey work when he hasn't.

I think the same thing happens with papyri. Prof. A thinks he can read something, and asks Prof. B for a second opinion. Prof. B has a quick look, and says, 'I think you may well be right.' When Prof. A advocates his theory to somebody else at the pub, he says that Prof. B agreed with him: but Prof. B didn't really agree, he just made encouraging noises …

If you are an eminent specialist and not being named, you are not putting your own reputation on the line, and may well prefer to be polite and encouraging. What counts is whether somebody agrees with you in print with their name at the bottom of the article …

RICHARD

Richard's eirenic explanation of professorial psychology reminds me of a friend's explanation of the notorious (and often misquoted) observation of Bishop Jenkins of Durham that the Resurrection was 'not just a conjuring trick with old bones'. The bishop was previously a professor; 'the trouble is', said my friend, 'he thinks that the Gentlemen of the Press are bright undergraduates who need stimulating'.

OLIVER NICHOLSON

After reading this piece, I tore open the plastic wrapping from today's just-delivered *Le Monde*. The subheading says: "'*C'est le seul buste connu de César réalisé de son vivant*," *annonce Luc Long*.' What worries me about M. Long is that when someone asks him at a party what he does for a living, he has to say, 'I am the principal heritage curator at the department of subaquatic and undersea research of the Ministry of Culture'.

MICHAEL BULLEY

I recently received the following letter from my old friend Hercule Poirot and in view of its importance in this matter I feel it should be made public.

My Dear Friend,

I 'av been reading the enormous number of comments concerning this discovery and am surprised that no one – no one –including the esteemed lady professor, has made, what to me is the most instantly obvious observation concerning it.

I ask you, *mesdames et messieurs*, to look carefully at this portrait bust and ask yourselves one simple question.

If I had a face like that, would I want it immortalised in stone for all time? Would my wife–colleagues–friends, on passing it each time they came to dinner, look on it reverently and say in hushed tones, 'What a great–noble–handsome–sensitive man your husband–senator etc. was'?

The answer *mes amis* is clearly, No!

Only if – only if – *mes amis*, the person depicted was so immensely, so enormously important that they agreed – indeed, that it was demanded of them – that they must be portrayed for all time for history as similarly as your Oliver Cromwell indicated, warts and naso-labials and all ...

This can therefore only be a bust of a very, very, very great man. And I am sure that my friends in the various French archaeology departments with their computerised facio-cranial measurements etc., will have confirmed that this is indeed Julius Caesar.

Some people have protested that no soldier would follow a man with such a face, but *messieurs*, the extreme depth of those naso-labials indicates a man of great endurance and ruthlessness, as Caesar was known to be.

Finally, may I suggest to the commenters, perhaps, a little less all-night raving and a little more use of those little grey cells.

Your Friend Hercule Poirot

LORD TRUTH

Are exams fair?

22 May 2008

I am on sabbatical leave and taking off to give a lecture in
Chicago while our students hone their skills by translating
Barack Obama and Milan Kundera into Latin and Greek. I kid
you not. In our day it was Macaulay or Churchill if you were
lucky (he was easier). But I guess that the effect of the Latin is
to make Obama sound much like Macaulay anyway.

It's hard to live through a summer term here without a
little nagging doubt about what exactly we are putting them
through the exam routine FOR. It's nowhere near as bad as the
school examining business which is currently getting itself tied
up in knots about accuracy and objectivity.

Their double bind is quite simple. The more kids you
examine, the more examiners you need. In the bad old days,
when we had only a small number of kids doing A level, then
we could afford to have wise and experienced examiners
evaluating exam answers about the relative merits of Gladstone
and Disraeli – with confidence.

The more kids take the exams, the harder it is to find
enough examiners (the pay is lousy), the less experienced
and qualified they will be overall (I don't mean individuals),
and the more we need to keep a careful eye on what exactly
they are getting up to. The totally safe way out is multiple
choice. Even a computer can mark that. If not multiple choice,
then every question has to come with a set of acceptable
answers handed out to each examiner. This lets you put even

trainee teachers into bat – all they have to do is match up the candidate's answer with their checklist.

The only trouble is that it stamps on imagination, independence and eccentricity, or on any poor child who has the nerve to mention a point not on the list. 'Not on the list' = 'no marks'. In the bad old days we relied on the wise and experienced to distinguish the eccentric and silly from the eccentric and brilliant. It's an inexact science, sometimes they made mistakes or weren't so wise and experienced after all, but we trusted them.

We haven't figured out how to have mass examining without a mechanistic approach to learning which in the end equals dumbing down.

Cambridge students are lucky by comparison.

We all accept that exams don't test every skill, and I suspect that there is a blokeish element to success in them (whether in women or men). So increasingly we use 'alternative methods of assessment' too, dissertations or portfolios of essays. But exams do test some skills we value. I, for one, am not knocking the acquisition of knowledge, useful memory, the ability to deploy learnt knowledge, to answer the question and to make a good argument. And our exams aren't bad at testing those things – as fairly as you could possibly hope.

Every exam script is marked anonymously. In the old days, you used to recognise the handwriting of the students you had taught, however 'anonymous' it was. But now you have most likely never seen your students' handwriting, so that problem has gone.

Each script is also marked by two people – first independently, then in consultation. I remember that, when I was a student, we used to worry hugely about the ideological differences between the two examiners. Would the trendy

Professor X mark you down for what the philological Professor Y would value? In my experience, both Professor X and Y are looking for students to answer well, under any ideological banner.

When examiners differ it is more often than not because one examiner has 'read' or 'understood' what the student was saying in different ways. Sometimes, honestly, when you talk to your fellow examiner, you see that you have just missed the student's point. Or the other examiner sees that he or she has given the kid too much benefit of the doubt. If you still don't agree, it can all be read by the external examiner. Yes, it's a time-consuming process.

OK, I can see that this tendency for examiners to agree might simply reflect an unspoken, unreflective collusion by a conservative academic establishment about what counts as 'good answers'. But I doubt it, honestly.

If any students are reading this, let me just say: stop worrying about all those arcane things that could go wrong – more marks are lost by NOT ANSWERING THE QUESTION than by any other failing at all.

Comments

Don't remind me about answering the question! I well remember an assignment I did some years ago. My tutor's comments started with 'This would have been an excellent essay if the question had been "Why Did the Romans Get Married?"'

JACKIE

Grading to a marking scheme in A levels was one of the worst experiences of my life: if your answer isn't there, nor are the marks. We were also instructed to accept certain 'wrong' answers, because a recommended text book contained errors.

ARMCHAIR PROFESSOR

Jackie – why did the Romans get married?

RICHARD

Richard – where would you like to start?! It was a few years ago, and I can't find the assignment (I think it's in the loft!) but I seem to remember the transfer of property figured quite a lot, and legitimate children. Political connections figured highly as well. And didn't Augustus bring in laws about people having to marry in an attempt to increase the population, and clean up morals? Or at least offering inducements to those that did. Certainly the last thing to be considered was female choices, though having three (I think) children gave the mother a degree of freedom which might have been tempting!

JACKIE

Exams are great. I always did well at most of the written ones. And my daughter has inherited the flair but also has a killer instinct for arguing/bullying teachers into submission that she gets from her mum. Since ability in the subject has almost nothing to do with it, and a good short-term memory and a bit of flash has everything, I think exams are perfect for turning out game-show producers and/or presenters.

XJY

MARY BEARD

They also teach one of the most valuable lessons one can take into life: Focus and ATFQ.

STEVE THE NEIGHBOUR

The Amy Winehouse exam

28 May 2008

I mentioned in passing last week that Cambridge Classics students had been honing their language skills by translating Milan Kundera and Barack Obama into Latin and Greek.

It didn't create quite the surge of interest that the Cambridge English practical critical question has – asking students to compare Walter Ralegh and Amy Winehouse. Bob Dylan and Billie Holiday were in the question, too, but no one got so steamed up about them. Perhaps the 'Dylan is the greatest poet since Shakespeare' campaign, by the eminent Christopher Ricks, has made him fair game for an exam.

But it is all part of the same phenomenon – which, *pace* the *Daily Mail*, is nothing to do with dumbing down.

When you teach a load of very bright students at Cambridge, one thing you want them to do is to be able to make connections, to think – cliché coming up, folks – 'out of the box'. That can sometimes mean encouraging them to use the critical rigour they have learned reading Tacitus, Shakespeare or whatever, in thinking about analogous, but unexpected phenomena of the here and now.

One of the most successful courses I ever ran was over fifteen years ago now. It was for third year classicists and historians in Cambridge, and was called 'The Roman Emperor: Construction and Deconstruction of an Image'. This was about the time of the protracted break-up of the marriage of Charles and Diana, enlivened for the world by the Squidgy- and Camilla-gate tapes. Remember?

The students read the tabloids, and the transcripts of the tapes, and the various biographies as they emerged. In at least one of the exams (the course ran for 3 years), a section of the paper was a gobbet test on part of the Camilla-gate tapes (all very carefully labelled 'An extract from the alleged conversation between HRH the Prince of Wales and Mrs Andrew Parker-Bowles ...')

No one from the *Daily Mail* complained (or noticed, I imagine). But some of the more staid members of the History Faculty were a bit dubious about getting their brightest-and-best to read Andrew Morton's biography of Di, let alone having a pirated phone conversation reprinted in the exam paper ... The staid classicists were more broad-minded, I should say.

But the result was explosive ... and enlightening.

There turned out to be all kinds of trade-offs in thinking about the tittle-tattle of ancient and modern monarchies. Why, we asked, was there such general interest in the eating (or non-eating) habits of the monarchs and royals? To what extent is that cross-cultural ... to what extent a narrowly particular Western tradition? Could thinking harder about our own obsessions throw light on antiquity, or not?

Then again, what counts as the words of the monarch, and how do we judge them? If we eavesdrop on a king/emperor, do we expect him to sound like us – or different? What are the conventions of royal speech? When (the alleged) 'Charles' used the word 'calumny' almost next to the word 'Tampax' (the only man in the history of the world ever to do so, I imagine), what did that tell us about the rhetoric of autocrats? How did Tacitus decide to invent the speech of emperors?

And, more to the point, could we explain how and why the internal goings on of a royal court actually mattered.

It wasn't dumbing down. There were no good marks for those who just squealed about Charles and Di. This was a course about putting together the ancient and modern. You needed to know your Tacitus and your Suetonius and your *Scriptores Historiae Augustae* backwards – and then to ask if there was any useful connection between them and the representation of the Windsors. One possible answer was 'no'.

As for that question in the English Tripos. It looks like a tough one to me:

> *The Oxford English Dictionary* defines 'lyric' as 'Of or pertaining to the lyre; adapted to the lyre, meant to be sung'. It also quotes Ruskin's maxim 'Lyric poetry is the expression by the poet of his own feelings'. Compare poem (a) on the separate sheet [a lyric by Sir Walter Ralegh, written 1592] with one or two of the song-lyrics (b)–(d) with reference to these diverse senses of 'lyric'.

'b–d' were lyrics by Winehouse ('Love is a Losing Game'), by Billie Holiday ('Fine and Mellow') and Bob Dylan ('Boots of Spanish Leather').

If anyone can imagine that this was a dumbed-down question, they should think again. Marks were not going to be given here for ranting on about AW and her troubles. This was about 'lyric', Ruskin, Ralegh ... and whichever modern star you chose. The kind of question that weak students know to avoid.

And if anyone thinks that Ms Winehouse is the most disreputable of the lot, they should go and take a closer look at the life of Sir Walter.

Comments

I know what they have in common: Walter Ralegh didn't give up his coke for anyone and Amy Winehouse didn't give up her cloak for anyone.

MICHAEL BULLEY

This is all very good news for the University of Oxford.

GEORGE

That paper isn't so much about what you 'study' as what you pick up along the way. It doesn't matter a jot if people were familiar with the passages or not – indeed, some of those who have read it all before (by some strange fluke) will have performed worse than people seeing them for the first time. And *vice versa*. And it really isn't that unusual for a practical criticism question, by all accounts.

NEWN1

Just because someone may be a 'drug-addled artist' doesn't mean they have nothing worthwhile to say.

STEVE KIMBERLEY

To paraphrase Porson on Robert Southey: 'Winehouse will be read – when Homer and Virgil are forgotten.'

SHAWCROSS

I was asked (in an exam) to translate into Latin a passage including the sentence 'in discourse he was stiff, awkward and angular' (Mommsen on Mark Antony, translated from German into English).

Nasty.

RICHARD

Examiners citing this person is really just another example of the present desperate attempts to get 'with it' (old slang) and reduce the apparent elitist view of Oxbridge.

You yourself make heroic efforts in this area endlessly referring to the seamier side of ancient life, and giving the impression that you are a semi drunk chain smoking old female lecher more suited to running a fifties bar in soho than gracing High Table. Of course we all realise that blogging is a relaxation from the intellectual pressures of ceaseless research, yet I notice that you carefully avoid anything that truly turns the stomach.

LORD TRUTH

To Richard: maybe 'in discourse he was stiff, awkward and angular' could be '*sermo autem horridus et rudis et impexus*'. *Impexus* (uncombed) may not quite get 'angular', but Tacitus uses it of speech, and I suppose that hair that hasn't been combed will be sticking out at all angles.

MICHAEL BULLEY

Why ruins are disappointing

5 June 2008

My next gig is in Paris – at a conference on ruins.

As almost always, two days in Paris in early June seemed a very nice idea when I agreed to give a paper last year. Whether the 6.30 a.m. Eurostar on Thursday seems quite such an attractive prospect now is another question.

It wasn't just Paris in the spring that made me say yes to the invitation. I've been brewing up a somewhat deviant view on ruins (academically deviant, that is) for some time.

Which is to say, I want to think a bit harder about why most ruins are – let's face it – disappointing.

I don't mean all ruins, of course. I challenge anyone to find Pompeii or the Parthenon or the Colosseum disappointing or boring (though, according to Peter Green, William Golding did mount the Athenian Acropolis, muttering, 'The bloody Parthenon again' and sat down firmly with his back to the monument gazing out at the Eleusis cement works). I mean those ivy clad mouldering walls of some third rate English abbey or the pile of stray stones outside some jolly Cretan village which claim to be the remains of a Minoan rural settlement.

To most people in the world, this disappointment will not seem a great revelation, but to archaeologists and cultural theorists ruins are an object of intense interest (and so they are to me when I am wearing one of those hats). Archaeologists will bang on for hours about the minute significance of the position of one stone against the next. Cultural theorists will bang on even longer about ruins as a metaphor for the past, the fragility of human success, the melancholy of contemplating the death of the past, and so on.

The voice that most academics refuse to hear is that of most other people in the world who do not share this enthusiasm. In fact, not to appreciate ruins or 'fragmentarity' is seen as a mark of boorish lack of comprehension. So, for example, when Benjamin Haydon overheard an ordinary member of the public say in front of the newly on-show Elgin Marbles, 'How broken down they are, a'ant they', he and most critics (me included) ever after have treated this as an example of naive ignorance.

In fact, not only is it absolutely true that they are very broken down (and disappointed many when they first arrived), but there was also a considerable move at the time to have them restored.

Even élite travellers could chime in to this effect (although we tend to prefer to linger over their enthusiasm for ruins). A friend put me on to a great passage of the nineteenth-century traveller William Forsyth, moaning about how difficult it was to make anything out of Hadrian's Villa at Tivoli: 'This villa was at first so diffuse, so deficient in symmetry or connexion, and is now so ruined, so torn by excavation, that its original plan is become an object extremely difficult for a stranger to recover.' And he goes on in the same vein with several paragraphs of complaint.

My point is going to be that we need to think harder about those on the anti ruin side – and to see them not as being indifferent to, or ignorant of, the past, but having a different way of engaging with it.

That might be helped by looking at those non-Western cultures who haven't bought into the romantic idea of ruins. Japan is an obvious example, where traditionally the 'oldest' temples were entirely rebuilt every 20 years or so (suggesting a view of history as process rather than material).

China is instructive, too, especially the recent debates about the restoration and rebuilding (or not) of the Garden of the Old Summer Palace (brutally destroyed in 1860 by the French and British, under the command of Lord Elgin, none other than the son of Lord 'Parthenon' Elgin). In this, we don't hear of the picturesque value of the 'garden as ruin' (and a very rundown ruin it is indeed). If there is a value in the ruin for the Chinese debaters, it is the ruin as 'evidence of Western atrocities … the scene of a crime'.

Not exactly how we see old Coventry cathedral?

Comments

I can never decide which is worse: my guilt as a lapsed Catholic walking past a church or my guilt as a former archaeology student lying by the pool in Crete and not visiting the ruins.

JAY

Surely if ruins are disappointing they are successful? If ruins actually fulfilled somebody's expectations, that would be a real disaster …

SW FOSKA

Yer can't get off on ruins in nice weather. What you are looking for in effect is to be moved in some ethereal way by the local environs and what you see. You need few people, you need grey skies and rain or snow, and you need to be in a thoroughly miserable and introverted state of mind to start with.

After all, you don't really enjoy sex unless you feel up for it, so why would you enjoy ruins unless you are totally emotionally receptive?

STEVE THE NEIGHBOUR

Why research is fun

11 July 2008

In the Cambridge University Library there's one predictable route to the unpredictable. It was the library's nineteenth-century practice to bind up short books and pamphlets together, perhaps as many as ten or twenty in a single volume. So you order up the thing you're wanting, and you get a load of what you weren't expecting, too.

The chances are that it's one of the other things that takes your fancy.

At least, that's what happened to me the other day. I was on the hunt for a short book called *The Comic History of Rome, and the Rumuns*, published in about 1847. When I do my lectures on laughter in Berkeley this autumn, I'm wanting to explore not just why the Romans laughed, but also why we laugh at the Romans. So this was obvious material.

But when the book arrived, it came bound up with nine others, two of which were just as interesting. One was a book I'm sure I ought to have known already, but didn't. It was called *Facetiae Cantabrigienses*, an 1820s collection of jokes and *bons mots* about Cambridge. What particularly caught my attention were not the anecdotes about Richard Porson, but the spoof exam papers, which were obviously the ancestors of the famous one in *1066 and All That* ('Do not write on both sides of the paper at once').

The questions went like this:

'Are you anywhere informed by Herodotus, which were the thickest, the heads of the Egyptians or the Persians?'

'Oxford must, from all antiquity, have been either somewhere or nowhere. Where was it in the time of Tarquinius Priscus ...?'

'Mention any instances that occur to you of ancients visiting any part of the United States ...'

'State logically how many tails a cat has.' (This one had a model answer, too. 'Cats have three tails – no cat has two tails – every cat has one tail more than no cat – *ergo*, every cat has three tails.')

OK – not side-splitting, I grant you. But it's hard to get much of an idea about how the takers thought about exams (classical or not) in the early nineteenth century. This kind of stuff is one way into their 'exam culture'.

The other was a satiric Lancashire dialect account of a visit to the Great Exhibition ... *O Full True un Pertikler Okeqwnt o wat me un maw mistris un yerd wi' gooin to th'Greyte Eggshibishun e'Lundun*. Satiric it may have been, but still a way of thinking differently about that extraordinary mid-Victorian spectacular.

There is another joke here. Both these rare books are available on Google Books. So I could have got them on my screen all along, without bothering to arm myself with a pencil (no pens in the Rare Books Room) and hoof off to the University Library.

But the fact is that I wouldn't have known about this if I hadn't ordered up the *Comic History* and flipped through the rest of the volume. That's where the UL and its funny nineteenth-century habits is always likely to score over Google Books.

Comments

When starting out in my career as an archaeologist, I started a research paper thus: 'Serendipity often plays a role in research. By sheer chance some piece of evidence turns up that fills a lacuna in current understanding.'

Perhaps not my finest opening two sentences, but I was accused of not taking the research process 'seriously enough'. When I asked my senior colleague whether he believed what I said to be true or downright nonsense, he said it might very well be true but that that was not the sort of statement to be making in a 'serious academic publication'.

THOMAS, LONDON

Heard the one about the Roman and the barber?

10 August 2008

I'm now full steam ahead on my Berkeley lectures about Roman laughter. And to be precise, off to spend the rest of Sunday in the library (thank heavens that our Faculty gives us access 24/7), for a side-splitting afternoon with some Roman jokes.

I've already given you some choice examples. But just for laughs, here's another favourite, from the collection known as the *Philogelos* (or 'Laughter-lover'):

> A man goes to get his hair cut by a talkative barber.
> 'How would you like your hair done?' asks the barber.
> 'In silence,' replies the man.

Not bad?

A good old-fashioned 2.1 is better than a Higher Education Achievement Record

27 October 2008

University examiners are an extremely conscientious crowd and, in my experience, degree marking is as fair as it could be, given human frailty (and far better that than a computer). All the same, I've often thought that we might be better off without the fixed degree class boundaries of first, 2.1, etc. As with all these linear classifications, it's hard to feel entirely happy about lumping together the person who just missed a first with the one who just scraped a 2.1, and so on. So I've always had a certain sympathy with the idea of introducing a more nuanced record of a university degree.

Until I saw what was being piloted as the 'Higher Education Achievement Record' (*Hear*, for short – of course), trumpeted in several papers this week. It is apparently being test run in several UK universities right now.

Reading about it, I was sent rushing back into the arms of the old conventional nineteenth-century system of 'classes', for all their faults. '*Hear*' has been developed by the kind of people who refer to what I call 'universities' as 'the sector' (that is, I guess, 'higher education sector'). Its well-meaning, market-oriented approach to grading represents another nail in the coffin of academic and intellectual values in the universities.

Why do they want to change?

Well, one reason, according to Bob Burgess (referring, proprietorially, to the work of 'my committee'), is that employers want more information than just a simple degree class (or projected one). Fine, but isn't that what references are for? I think of it as part of my job to write references for my students, written specially for the particular post they have in mind. The best way of ensuring potential employers ('stakeholders' in Burgess-speak) get useful input from me is simple. First, make sure the references I write are confidential; second, make sure that employers take them up before short-listing the candidates, not after. There is no record of achievement that can be as helpful as two conscientious references.

Another is the idea that the final degree class doesn't reflect the strengths and weaknesses shown by a student throughout the course. Thank heavens it doesn't, I think. I am privileged to teach some of the very brightest students in the UK. I want them to develop their potential in all kinds of ways – so that, in whatever walk of life, they can go on to be stunning citizens (cliché but true). That often means taking apart their preconceptions. It means watching them take intellectual risks, make intellectual mistakes, even do badly before they do really well. The last thing I want is every course they have done listed and graded. That's a recipe for the US climate, where the students are knocking on your door complaining if you don't give them an A. For there every mark counts. Some of my best students in Cambridge have got deltas on the way to alphas, and have learnt in the process about how not to be yes-women, when and how to take risks. Isn't that what UK employers need?

The worst bit of this is the spectre of the extra-curricular activities that may get included on the report. The very last thing we need is every student rushing off to be president of a society to get it on their transcript. For a start, who is to say whether they have been a GOOD president or not? I've been through enough UCAS interviews (and yes, interviews ARE useful) where I've said to a potential student: 'Oh I see you're president of your school Tibetan society, what does that involve?' 'Well, we haven't actually met yet,' comes the answer. But the more important point is that students learn to become good citizens (they learn to grow up, in other words) in many different ways. Some do it by beavering around running societies; others do it by lying on their beds for long hours listening to Bob Dylan and thinking. No one, believe me, can predict which has the better outcome. But I do know that among the best contributors to the twenty first century are some on-the-bed Bob Dylan listeners.

We don't need *Hear*s, sectors, or Burgess reports. We need university teachers with the space to get to know their students and to write for them honestly, supportively and appropriately, whatever their degree result.

Comments

I hope that a few robust vice-chancellors will point out that, just as it is not the job of universities to do social engineering, it is not their job to serve employers. Can we club together to send copies of Matthew Arnold's *Culture and Anarchy* and John Henry Newman's *The Idea of a University* (specifically part 1, discourse 5) to a few government ministers?

RICHARD BARON

'But I do know that among the best contributors to the twenty-first century are some on-the-bed Bob Dylan listeners.'

Hear, hear! I finally have an advocate.

JOHN T

I think Cambridge should close any student society that advertises itself by putting 'IT WILL LOOK GOOD ON YOUR CV' anywhere whatsoever on their promotional material!

STEFAN

It's bonkers to ban Latin

2 November 2008

I was contacted last week by a *Telegraph* journalist. The *Telegraph* had uncovered, he said, the fact that local councils were banning Latin words from all official documents and in their dealings with the public more generally. This was information the paper had obtained using the Freedom of Information Act. (Hang on … do you really need the FOI Act to find out about this, or did the horrid truth emerge during a trawl for something even more sinister?)

What was my reaction? Well, at first thought, it was a bit mixed. It looked like another of those pseudo-populist gestures that councils and government are in the habit of making. They make you fill in a form 20 pages long to claim some tiny benefit you are entitled to … then they congratulate themselves for the whole document being entirely 'Latin-free'. Humbug. On the other hand, there are some Latin phrases I don't have too much affection for. I wouldn't shed many tears for '*nil obstat*', for example.

But when I discovered what the offending words were, the only conclusion was that the whole scheme was bonkers – and ignorant.

The list of words for the chop included not only *ad hoc* and *prima facie*, but e.g., *vice versa*, i.e. and NB.

As I huffed to the *Telegraph* man, this is a dreadful example of ethnic cleansing applied to language. And, what is more, it totally misunderstands the nature of the English language which is 'English' precisely by virtue of it being very mixed indeed, as much 'foreign' as it is 'native', indeed more so. 'NB' is now as much English as it was ever Latin. In fact, it has much wider currency and usage in modern English than it ever did in antiquity.

What will be left, I wonder, when they turn their attention to other 'foreign' words No RSVP, or bungalow, rendezvous or karaoke. The list is endless.

Meanwhile, the overworked functionaries at benighted Bournemouth Council are busy thinking up clunky English equivalents for all this nasty Latin. The neat adjectival '*ad hoc*' is to be replaced by 'for this special purpose'. Similar time is being wasted in Fife (where '*ex officio*' has bit the dust) and Salisbury.

Oh well, I expect they will have a bit of fun when they get on to '*flagrante delicto*' (and they might at the same time then realise that this kind of English had its points).

Comments

That'd be the end of nineteenth century English Lit. for a start.

Maybe they should try banning French and German imports, and the people using them: '*Honi soit qui mal y pense*' and '*Ich dien*'.

XJY

Well done, Bournemouth.
Progress cannot wait.
Give us proper English
For those Latin words we hate.
Do you need translators?

For Latin's what I know.
But I can't do it for nothing.
What's the thing of roughly the same value that I'd get in
    return?

MICHAEL BULLEY

No doubt the Bournemouth Council think '*vis-a-vis*' is Latin for
'strength from strength'.

JAY DILLON

Barack Obama – and the first 'African-Roman' emperor of Rome

18 November 2008

I'm surprised that no one seems to have spotted an obvious Roman parallel for the success of Barack Obama. Or have I missed it? In the second century AD, Lucius Septimus Severus became the first 'African-Roman' emperor of Rome. Like Obama he was of mixed race – his father from Libya, his mother of European descent. He too had an outspoken and determined wife, from Syria. And his first task on coming to the throne in 193 AD was to deal with a military disaster in Iraq ('Parthia', as it was then known). The success of his surge was commemorated in the great arch, which remains to this day one of the most impressive monuments in the Forum at Rome.

The two little children he took with him to the palace did not fare so well. In fact they grew up to be murderous thugs – even if the elder, Caracalla, did go on to initiate the most daring extension of civil rights in the whole of world history. Once he had got rid of his brother (nastily murdered on his mother's lap), he gave full Roman citizenship, and the legal privileges and protection that went with it, to all the free male inhabitants of the empire.

Did the success of Septimius Severus show that race no longer mattered in Roman politics? And is there a message in his story for the new president-elect?

If so, the message is a double-edged one. A few more African-Romans did make it to the higher echelons of the imperial government (in many cases members of the emperor's own family, or his wife's friends). But on the wider view, it was not so much that his race did not matter, but that the Roman upper class and the Roman media made sure that it simply was not seen.

We do not know for certain whether or not Septimius Severus was black. That is itself significant. One historian writing three hundred years after his lifetime claimed that he was 'dark', and one or two portrait statues appear to show him with African features. But the vast majority of images that survive make him look like any other Roman emperor before him – his whiteness over-emphasised by the shiny white marble in which he was so often portrayed. This was not a black man claiming the imperial throne for himself. This was the Roman imperial machine turning a man of colour into an emperor more or less indistinguishable from all his predecessors. The machine was making sure that race did not show.

No one is suggesting, of course, that Obama's publicity team will attempt, literally, to whiten the image of the forty-fourth president. But the 'Septimius Severus problem' is already clear enough. Obama's understandable decision not to mention his own ethnic identity, or anything else about race, in his acceptance speech had decided echoes of Septimius Severus' image as a white emperor. The more you present Obama as any other president, and peddle the self-congratulatory clichés about the end of a racial divide at the highest pinnacle of American politics, the more you are simply refusing to see that for most people in the US and the rest of the world race does still matter...

Most British women will recognise a much more recent political analogy. For ethnicity, read gender. Margaret Thatcher did almost nothing to advance the chances of other women in British public life, quite the reverse. By making it look as if the gender wars were a conflict now decisively won – when for millions of British women the battle had hardly begun – the effect of Thatcher's victory was to put back the cause of women for a generation at least.

Let's hope the same is not true for Obama – and that he doesn't take the Septimius Severus route towards the same old orthodoxy of power. If race (or gender) is really not to matter it needs to be visible to us.

Comments

If Severus' father was a Libyan (and not, as I had always assumed, descended from Romans who had settled in Libya), then he would have been half Berber (possibly with some Greek mixed in). As such, he would not really have been all that dark, a bit swarthy perhaps, and his features would not really have demonstrated what we think of as African (i.e. sub-Saharan) characteristics. In any case, he would not have been black as Americans understand the term. (I believe the British use the word somewhat more broadly.) Still, it would be interesting to know how the Romans painted his statues.

DEMETRIOSX

Is this a troll? Can a Professor in Classics at Cambridge seriously attempt to offer such twisted pseudo-logic, half-truths, speculation and personal desire as fact?

This laughable conspiracy theory that Mary Beard puts forth: that some seemingly vast number of Romans were engaged in a racist cover-up of their emperor's very appearance is an example of the worst sort of revisionist drivel.

MARK

Suggesting that a Roman emperor's image (as represented in statues, etc.) was carefully manipulated is not a 'laughable conspiracy theory': it is a statement of the bleeding obvious … I have no idea whether Septimius was or was not 'black' (the word's connotations in any case obviously different then from now, regardless of what kind of skin pigmentation is being described); but it isn't a silly question whether this was emphasised, ignored or suppressed.

RICHARD

Don't forget that painted wooden tondo of Septimius and his family. If this circular panel was produced in Egypt (as Hiesinger thinks), then the colouring of the figures may not tell you very much. If you look at a random selection of paintings on tomb walls, you will see men and women both dark and light. I have often wondered if this has to do with the paint available at the time of painting.

Your (not very seriously meant, I take it) point highlights the pitfall of trying to match up the modern world with the ancient world. An example of this came to my attention several years ago when I heard a geographer on Laurie Taylor's programme claiming that Jesus was born on the West Bank. Even though it was radio, you could hear the capital letters. He was born in an area which was then and still is on the west bank of the Jordan river.

ANTHONY ALCOCK

Oxbridge interviews: real advice from a real don

8 December 2008

This week marks the start of the Oxbridge interview season. I've been watching with interest from the USA as newspapers peddle advice to anxious applicants and their parents about how they might best get through the ordeal – and especially about how to deal with all those weird questions that we dons do like to devise to trip up the poor candidates.

More often than not, the information is being fed to the press by Oxbridge Application Advisory companies, which make their money out of increasing the Oxbridge mystique, then claiming to offer a way through the applications jungle.

Feel some sympathy for Oxford and Cambridge, please. While we do our best to demystify the process and explain why interviews are useful (can *you* think of a better way of distinguishing two students, both with 10 A*s at GCSE and predicted four As at A level?), other people have a financial stake in making it all seem as complicated as possible.

One company is charging £950 for an interview preparation weekend, which is just one small part of the 'Premier Service' (covering everything from advice on your personal statement to 14 hours' personal tuition to promote independent thinking), for which they don't even quote a price on the web; you have to phone, which I haven't. I can't imagine the price is far short of the just over £3000 annual fees for being taught at Cambridge. To be fair to this company, you *can* apply for their access scheme, a much shorter version, if you receive Educational Maintenance Allowance – though how many people are given this is not clear. Perhaps it depends on how many spare places they have once the fee-payers have paid their fees.

So what is my advice?

OK, I can't speak for science subjects, but for humanities – three things.

First, don't worry about the weird questions. We don't sit round each year and dream them up over the port (port – another myth, for the most part). 'I know, Humphrey, why don't we ask them if they can imagine what it was like being a strawberry … That'll sort the sheep from the goats, eh?'

If the questions sound a bit unexpected, that is what they are meant to be. It's partly to prevent people being drilled in the 'right answer' at ambitious schools or on those fee-paying courses. So don't be misled by all those people who try to tell you that what 'they' are really after when they ask you 'How does Geography relate to *A Midsummer Night's Dream*' ('a wonderful chance to show you can adopt an interdisciplinary approach'). It really isn't like that. Worse still, don't try to second-guess what the agenda is. Engage in the conversation, trusting that the person asking the question is trying to get the best out of you.

Second, ask yourself: what would *I* be looking for in an applicant for this subject to this university? The application process isn't rocket science. If someone asks you what you have read about your chosen subject outside of your A level syllabus, and you say 'Nothing', it's not a great start. Arts courses at Oxbridge demand huge amounts of reading and an engagement with the written word. Be able to talk about something you have read, independently, that has engaged

you, whether it's a battered 1950s text book you found in the
chuck out pile at the school library, or a 3 for 2 offer at W. H.
Smith.

Third, don't put your faith in profit-making companies that
promise to help you 'get in', and claim that they have advice
from sources close to the mysterious decision-making. (Sorry
– if you already have shelled out vast amounts of money, it
probably hasn't actually done you any harm, but there might
have been better ways of spending your money!) No one I
know who is really close to the admissions process would sell
themselves to a private company.

I took a look at the 'Advisory Board' of one of these
organisations. The descriptions were strictly accurate, but still
gave a misleading impression of intimacy with the system.
One of the advisers was described as 'a former schoolteacher
Fellow of Magdalene, Cambridge, specialising in admissions'.
OK, but 'schoolteacher Fellows' are teachers who come to a
college for a term, on sabbatical from a school. They may have
an interest in admissions, but they have nothing at all directly
to do with them. Another had been involved in admissions in
a 'Permanent Private Hall' at Oxford (which is not quite the
same as a college). Another was an interesting cultural theorist
– who most likely had once been involved in admissions at a
post-graduate college at Oxford, but I couldn't discover which
exactly (Google was a bit unclear on this).

Why not instead take advantage of what is available outside
the commercial sector? The Sutton Trust arranges courses
with an eye to Oxbridge and to other top-rank universities
(Oxbridge isn't the be-all and end-all). A friendly teacher
can almost certainly help to get you a practice interview (and
honestly, you don't need a whole weekend of it).

In fact, the Cambridge website gives you an example of what an interview is like; and it's made by those who REALLY know. I'd start there.

Comments

This post has made me feel a lot better about being in the minority of Oxbridge applicants who HAVEN'T been to one of these interview weekend things – nearly everyone at my school seems to have paid for some kind of preparation!

So thank you for allowing me to have more faith in my decision of spending the time I would have used at a preparation weekend reading, and the money on shoes ...

And thank you for calming my nerves this morning, as I'm about to leave for my first Cambridge interview!

ANON

When you do these weekends, you are only getting what people at good private schools get as a matter of course. A friend of mine who went to Brighton College while Seldon was in charge got put through about seven mock interviews each more frightening than the next. With teachers they didn't know. What good practice, compared to someone who's never done anything like it.

And we definitely got similar help at my school. Whereas a girl I know who had gone to a private, but unacademically ambitious Steiner school, finally got into Oxford (second time round) after taking one of the courses you are discussing. She felt it was worth every penny.

PS At my interview I knelt in front of the door and listened through the oak to the person before me getting grilled. He was having a Middle East peace process nightmare.

When I got in there, the famous expert on Italian politics put on a slightly jazzy record, told me to sit down, offered me a grape, and said, 'Do you have any questions for me?' … Sometimes I think they have made up their mind before you get there …

EMMA T

I did well enough at the interview to be asked back for a second chance, at which I made it, despite my cheap suit and naivety and coming from a Middlesbrough school with no Oxbridge record and not even knowing our Latin master had been to the very college I was applying for (about which he was quite peeved). And I can't remember any weird questions. All I can remember is quoting some poem in French and not knowing what 'trite' meant (after a bit of close reading/*explication de texte*).

So not to worry. Competition has probably got more professional/slicker since then, but brains haven't.

XJY

I can't remember much about my interview with you except being asked about women in the classical world and at the turn of the century. The question horrified me, having given up history in Year 9 … but you still let me in and for this I am extremely grateful!

RUTH P

Hm, as an ex-Oxford student now teaching at Cambridge, I can vouch that what MB says sounds spot-on to me. During my DPhil I did a lot of exam coaching for slacker teenagers with rich parents: in not one case did it make a blind bit of difference. The bright ones remained bright, the thick ones stayed thick and did not get in.

MARK W

I think you're probably right about the port being a myth. I phoned an old friend on Sunday who decided to settle in Oxford after his many teaching stints abroad and he told me that dinner in college was pretty well a thing of the past. Lunch, he said, was a quasi-business meeting, with 'people exchanging papers over the shepherd's pie' and only water to drink. My guess is that many of the younger dons don't even know what port is. Reminds me of Basil Fawlty (complaining about a socially inferior guest): 'Wouldn't know the difference between a claret and a Bordeaux.'

ANTHONY ALCOCK

At High Table in my college – where I believe MB has dined on occasion – the port certainly isn't a myth!

MARK W

OK, Mark ... there is some occasional port hidden away in Cambridge nooks.

MARY

Whether or not port's a myth, I was offered sherry by one of my Oxford interviewers. Mind you, that was over thirty years ago. I almost fainted from delight at the perfection of it all – comfy room, chatting about *Paradise Lost* as we sipped, and there was even a fluffy cat on a cushion. I wasn't accepted, though.

RUTH

What's in a don's inbox?

18 December 2008

Remember those 'inbox' tests they used to make people do at job interviews? The candidate was sat down in front of a made-up collection of letters, notes and demands that might be lying in their inbox on their first day in the job and asked to prioritise! The idea was to see if they would rank buying the boss's wife an anniversary present in front of fixing up a meeting with the managing director. I was never quite sure what the right answer was supposed to be … or if there was one.

Well, I thought you might be interested to see what a real life donnish inbox looked like: the electronic version, I mean. California is a good place for reflecting on one's email. By the time you get up in the morning most of the European messages for the day are already waiting for you.

So, what does the gathered harvest of yesterday look like? It was in fact rather a thin crop. It's nearly Christmas and well past the end of term – so there were none of the usual apologies/excuses for students ('Sorry – my essay WILL be in your pigeonhole by 5.00, Susie xxxxxxx') and the usual administrative stuff of the working week. So treble this for the mid-term picture.

First in the box was good news …

1   An email from a friend who has just been appointed to be Director of the American Academy in Rome. A nice comment, I reflected, on passing years. I remember when we got all

excited because our friends had got *scholarships* there. Now they're becoming the bloody director ...

2 Domestic note from the husband. Largely concerned with delivering the 90th birthday card to my old teacher.

3 *Ditto.*

4 *Ditto* – plus re. the vegetable order.

5 Message from BBC World Service about an interview I'm doing next week on Google Earth's Ancient Rome, confirming time and place.

6 Message from Oundle Literary Festival wanting attractive donnish photo of self for their programme.

7 Copy of message from husband to colleague in Canada, where we are both going in the spring for a couple of lectures.

8 Message from editor and fellow blogger, to whom I'd sent the draft of a long review that I wasn't very happy with. He thought it needed more work too. (Damn – you always faintly hope that someone else might just think it brilliant, even if you don't yourself.) In this case the problem is that I'm too close to the subject, so it gets a bit anal. Looking at it again I decided that I needed to start from the anecdote I ended with (isn't that always the way?) ... so that's the job for the airport this afternoon.

9 PS note from fellow blogger re. my newly austere, healthy, weight-losing lifestyle. The truth is that redoing that review might well test the resolve.

10 Message from blog reader in Germany with intriguing query about Latin love stories. I'm always happy to get these – so long as they are not the kind of queries that could easily

be answered by a quick Google trawl. So I send off a speedy response.

11 Message from friend about recent blog post. 'Causing trouble again,' he said.

12 Query from student at another UK university asking me if I thought that Roman institutions owed a lot to the Etruscans. It was a follow-up question to something I had written, so I banged off a reply.

13 Confirmation of Canada arrangements.

14 Copy of message sent around the members of the Cambridge Leverhulme project I'm involved with. They are going on an outing to the British Museum and can't quite work out whether the 7.45 train from Cambridge will get them there in time (academics ...!)

15 Confirmation of confirmation of Canada.

16 More train stuff.

17 An email containing a link to a pdf of something I'm meant to be reading for a meeting in January.

18 Message forwarded from the husband – a weird complaint about his Byzantium show at the Royal Academy.

19 Christmas greetings from the European Research Council.

20 More train stuff.

21 Message from the *National Geographic*. I had given them a blog entry about the most important discovery of 2008. They don't think Obama counts as a discovery, so can I suggest something else? I have a quick search and send them Augustus' house on the Palatine.

22 Circular message from Cambridge Faculty Administrator, telling us all that our '800th Anniversary' lapel pins are in our pigeonholes. I haven't a clue what these are, but assume that someone has had the bright corporate idea that all Cambridge staff will celebrate the uni's birthday by wearing a badge. Not likely.

23 Message from friend to say that we can't meet when I hoped.

24 Message from San Francisco radio station who want to fix up a discussion about Pompeii from Cambridge (yes odd, I know, when am in SF).

25 More train stuff.

26 *Ditto*.

27 *Ditto*.

28 Pdf of wonderful pictures for a piece on Pompeii in the magazine *Historically Speaking*.

29 Query from student in Ireland interested in the Cambridge Classics MPhil. Wrote straight back with some answers.

By this time my hard work at clearing was beginning to be self-defeating. For numbers 30 and 31 were replies from numbers 10 and 12.

If anyone would like to tell me what all this says about modern electronic life, I'd love to know.

RAE madness

21 December 2008

As every university teacher and administrator in the UK knows, the results of the Research Assessment Exercise were announced last Thursday. The reaction since then has been fairly sick-making, especially from those who came well out of this dreadful process.

Me included, I'm afraid. According to most calculations, Cambridge came out 'top' overall (unless you use a different method of calculation, which lands the LSE at the top of the table). And in the Classics race alone, Cambridge came top, 'beating' Oxford by a whisker. And yes, I'll 'fess up, I have shared a self-satisfied smile or two about that with colleagues here since I got back.

But hang on. Have we all forgotten what a dreadful process this is? And isn't it the responsibility of those who have done well out of it to speak out loudest against it? For them, at least, it doesn't look like sour grapes.

Now, I don't mean to insult all those hardworking academics (over a thousand of them) who gave up weeks of their time to assess the submitted work (and make the process as fair as it could be). And I don't mean to insult all my colleagues in Cambridge who spent years trying to make sure that our submission was as good as possible. In fact, I'm really grateful to them. Besides, I was on my own Faculty's RAE committee and spent many hours strategising.

But let's remember that the real point of this exercise is to divide up inadequate research resources under the cover of 'objectivity'. But how objective can it ever be – when the main element of the process involves grading each of up to four 'outputs' written by every academic 'lucky' enough to be entered into one of four/five grades: 4* – world-leading in terms of originality, significance and rigour; 3* – internationally excellent in terms of originality, significance and rigour, but which none the less falls short of the highest standards of excellence; 2* – recognised internationally in terms of originality, significance and rigour; 1* – recognised nationally in terms of originality, significance and rigour; and 'unclassified' – falling below the standard of nationally recognised work, or outside the guidelines in some way.

OK, there must be some open and shut cases, but an awful lot must be much closer calls between 4*, 3* or even 2*. And if we knew the individual gradings, I bet there would be some we would take issue with.

And this is not to mention the vast amounts of university time and resources that went into trying to figure out how to work the system best (would it be financially better in the end to submit more academics, even if the average 'score' went down?), assembling all the information, writing the department's statement about itself, and chasing up all the submissions which had to be sent off to the RAE HQ somewhere.

And it's not to mention either the nasty culture of competition that resulted, as strategic appointments were made – and anxious deans put pressure on anxious heads of department, who then put pressure on their overworked staff to come up with another book ... It's no secret that all this chased some people out of the profession, and made others terminally miserable.

Less discussed are the bigger changes of academic culture that have resulted. In particular, there is now a tremendous pressure and incentive to *publish* – and no longer much sense that it might be possible to have a good idea *without* getting in print. There is too much publishing going on in British academic life, not too little – and that has been encouraged by the RAE.

Just to make matters worse, most newspaper accounts have failed to get to the bottom of the complicated grading system in use. The results came for each department (I mean 'Unit of Assessment') under 5 heads, with the percentage of 'outputs' submitted by each department awarded each of the 5 grades (with some adjustment for various other factors also taken into account and which are far too complicated to explain). My own Faculty scored like this: 4^* – 45%; 3^* – 25%; 2^* – 30%; 1^* 0%.

That does NOT mean what many newspapers thought it meant – that 45% of Cambridge classicists were world leading (though that might also be true!). It means that 45% of the individual submissions (up to 4 per academic) were judged world leading. Most of us will have made submissions that were given different ratings – our 'big book' maybe getting a 4^*, a more popular book something 'lower', etc., etc.

In my case, as I remember, I submitted my Triumph book, my Parthenon book, an article on Cicero's letters and an article on William Ridgway. I would (now I've seen the figures) be a bit surprised if the Triumph didn't get a 4^*, but the Parthenon was a book with a lot of research behind it aimed at a more general audience – which should *not* have got a 4^* (but was nevertheless an important contribution – I think – for an academic to make).

Oh well, this is the last RAE. The trouble is that its replacement (which almost certainly will be more mechanistic) will almost certainly be worse.

Comments

Mary, I too work in a shit-hot department. And it's true, there are nutty elements of the system. But don't you agree that there must be some form of evaluation of research? and that this must involve some form of 'better' or 'worse' measurement? and that this may as well involve numbers as not?

The new system will indeed be worse. Points will be awarded for amount of research income awarded. So if I write an article on Cicero with the aid of a 500000 pound grant, it's *de facto* better than your article on Cicero, if you did yours without a grant. It's like giving an art prize on the basis of the quantity of paint amassed by the artist rather than on the artwork.

SW FOSKA

Might we not be just as well off with a system in which judgements as to who got what did not have to be justified (so that there were no long reports to write), but we relied on the wisdom of crowds? This would be like the free market, where we all make our purchasing decisions but are not required to justify them.

First decide how much to spend on a given discipline in total, for the whole country. Give each professor or lecturer in the discipline a list of all of the institutions, except his or her own, showing the number of staff in the discipline at each institution. Ask each professor or lecturer to say how the funds for the discipline should be spread across all of the institutions. Average the results. There is the answer. The inability to allocate funds to one's own institution would work against the larger departments, but so long as there were a fair few large departments, that effect should not be too bad, and if it were, an adjustment could be made.

My reservation is that the wisdom of crowds, whether as a general principle or in precise mathematical guises such as the Condorcet Jury Theorem, only works if the members of the crowd make their choices independently. I have heard a malicious rumour that academics gossip to one another. That could undermine their independence in this exercise.

RICHARD BARON

There are many just criticisms that can be made of the RAE, but the claim that it has led academics to publish too much is surely not one of them. After all, the maximum that can be submitted to the RAE is four articles; and there are surely very few academics – either in the UK or anywhere else – who don't publish at least 4 articles over each 7-year period!

RALPH WEDGWOOD

So learned academics would not have admitted Socrates to their universities and fully justified their arbitration by several different and competing bureaucratic arguments. Curious world.

FEATHERSTONEHAUGH

Underwater Romans

25 December 2008

Sometimes it's hard to keep up with new Roman discoveries. I would like to blame my own single-minded attention to Pompeii, and then to Roman laughter. But the particular discoveries I've got interested in today were made several years ago – so I just can't have been paying attention.

An archaeological friend of the husband who came to pre-Xmas lunch on Tuesday pointed us to the Comacchio shipwreck, not far from where he usually lives.

Comacchio, near Ferrara, is a kind of mini Venice, built on thirteen little islands connected by bridges. And in the late 1980s, as I now know, the remains of an ancient boat were discovered near the city, in an area that had once been an ancient beach. The boat had run aground in the first century BC and been covered with the sand.

What intrigued me were the contents of this vessel. They included not just the usual kind of cargo: in this case amphorae, pottery, logs of boxwood, over 100 Spanish lead ingots (many stamped with the name Agrippa), plus the usual bric-à-brac for a voyage (tools, clothes, sandals, etc.). There were also 6 small lead portable shrines, in the shape of mini temples, of a sort I've never seen before. Some have mini images of Mercury in them, others Venus.

Were they cargo intended for sale? Were they picked up somewhere to be flogged back home (perhaps a bit of commercial speculation … someone spots them on sale and reckons he can sell them for profit back home). That seems more likely than that the set were all part of the crew's personal possessions. Either way, it seems like a striking piece of Roman evidence for what may well have been a personal religious object, and so personal religious devotion. Or were they elegant ornaments without much active religious significance at all?

Anyway, I soon found myself on the trail of more Roman boats.

No fewer than 16 Roman boats (dating from the second century BC to the fifth AD) have recently been discovered at what was the ancient river port of Pisa, wrecked in the harbour. I'd missed these, too, despite a few reports in British newspapers, as I have now realised.

The cargoes of these are no less striking. One, which seems to have come from north Africa, had a lioness on board, as well as three horses. Another came from south Italy, carrying peaches, cherries, plums and walnuts in re-used amphorae (their improvised stoppers were made of fragments of marble statues and bits of Vesuvian lava). There were even remains of a crew member, too: the skeleton of a man in his forties, with a dog.

At this point the husband had something to add, because he is just back from Istanbul, where he had seen the excavations of the Byzantine harbour. Here over 30 boats have been discovered. As well as lots of evidence for the harbour installations – plus skeletons of horses, presumably used to cart the cargo (vast quantities of wine, to judge from the smashed amphorae) away on dry land.

Anyway, that's what has been keeping me amused and away from what I should be doing over the last day or so. Now, in just a few hours, it's off to get the turkey, stuffing, etc. in the oven.

Happy Christmas everyone.

Comments

It's always irked me to hear other men talk of 'the wife' – nice to hear 'the husband' for a change.

DAVID MOORCRAFT

David Moorcraft may be interested to learn that I have already begun to restore the correct reading 'the husband' in place of 'my husband' in the whole of English literature. I decided to make a start with Shakespeare. And so we now have, for example, in *The Comedy of Errors*, 'Neither the husband nor the slave return'd', and, in *Richard III*, 'When he that is the husband now'. I nearly missed 'he so takes on yonder with the husband' from *Merry Wives of Windsor*. It looks like being a long task.

MICHAEL BULLEY

It's a don's life – the book

31 December 2008

This is the last post before the end of 2008 and a piece of news (OK – a confession) to share with you.

There is more than a chance that a selection of *A Don's Life* posts will be gathered together into that old-fashioned thing called a BOOK, coming out next autumn. You and I may share some initial anxieties about whether a blog translates well into print media. But the team at Profile Books convinced me that the answer was yes. Or, at any rate, worth a try.

If you've got any favourite posts that you think might get missed, let me know.

Now, the next question is about the comments – because I think that they give this blog its distinctive character.

My line has always been that a blog is about dialogue. So the plan is to include a few comments, certainly not a huge number, to capture that character.

Anyway, while you're reading this, I'm in Sudan … practising my Arabic, visiting the daughter, seeing the antiquities of Khartoum and around, and celebrating my 50-somethingth birthday.

On all of which, more soon.

Comments

I am happy to go on record as saying 'Prof. Beard is wonderful – I want to be just like her when I grow up – her blog is one of the best around, and her books are pretty cool too'.
DOROTHY KING

A book of blog contributions would be another example of the ephemeral being treated as the lasting and valuable – a mere piece of bookmaking. If Dorothy King really took Mary Beard's contributions to Classics seriously she would have put her books first.
PETER WOOD

In the book version will all the apostrophes be added to the donts, wonts and cants? You could view this as a public health issue. Regular readers of these pieces know to grit their teeth gently to anticipate a rise in blood pressure, but some unsuspecting soul, buying the book on a whim, might be overwhelmed by a lot of donts all in one go. I hear the ambulance siren already. Or will historical accuracy and the author's preference be respected? I'm assuming that slips that are not part of Mary Beard's idiograph (coined word) will be corrected: I noticed bosses for boss's a couple of blogs ago, for example. In view of the origin of these pieces (blogs, rather than carefully checked articles), I'd say the publishers needed the services of a top-class proofreader, who would spot things you wouldn't normally expect to find in an MS. Good practice dictates that the checking should not be left to the author. Even authors who are eagle-eyed when it comes to mistakes in other people's work are likely to overlook things in their own (you read what you thought you wrote rather than what you did).

MICHAEL BULLEY

[Ed. writes: We took Michael Bulley's point and corrected (i.e. added) the apostrophes. He had earlier made the same point with this ditty:

'Apostropoem'
When Mary Beard writes 'cant',
It's not the word that rhymes with 'rant'.
And when she writes a 'dont',
It isn't French. It's just her wont.]

I am intrigued to know what arguments from Profile Books allayed your initial anxieties about this *propositum haud necessarium*.

NICHOLAS WIBBERLEY

The book-from-the-blog reads like a cool idea, go for it!

GI

I had a feeling it might come to something like this. It will be interesting now to see what effect the prospect of inclusion will have, whether in terms of reticence or elaborate garrulousness in an effort to get noticed. But, included or not, we are supposedly being read by thousands. Maybe it is fame, at last.

FG

Afterword

I was, at first, a reluctant blogger. Now, after three years 'on the blog', blogging has become part of my life. It would, in fact, be hard to imagine life without it.

In early 2006, I was one of those writers scooped up by newspapers and magazines (in my case, *The Times Literary Supplement*) and invited to contribute blogs to their new on-line editions. The deal was that, for a modest recompense, I was to provide two posts per week on subjects that would include university life at Cambridge and the ancient Greeks and Romans – though books, arts, modern politics and the occasional rant were welcome too.

The title was to be *A Don's Life* and, as I soon discovered, I was to be billed as 'a wickedly subversive commenter on both the modern and the ancient world'. Three years on, I would happily shed the 'wickedly subversive' label. (How could anyone who appears to describe *themselves* as 'subversive' really be so? And how could anyone go on being 'subversive' year after year?) But I am afraid that the label has stuck. That is how I am now regularly introduced when I give lectures and talks, even when the sober topic of Roman history I am addressing has nothing subversive about it whatsoever.

At the time I was made the offer, I had never knowingly read a blog – but this didn't stop me having predictable academic prejudices about the whole genre. I thought that blogs were too immediate, too thoughtless and often too short to have anything serious to contribute to the world; they were

another step in the downward spiral of British journalism and
comment. I also suspected that having a blog was the literary
equivalent of tourism with a camera. Like the tourist in search
of the photo rather than the experience, I was afraid that I
would start to see life in terms of blogging opportunities.
(Wrong, said the *TLS* editor, when I raised the problem;
blogging would become a good excuse to do things I wouldn't
otherwise have done.)

So why on earth did I say yes and start the blog? There are
two simple answers. First, subversive or not, I usually do what
editors ask – or, at least, I'm ready to give their suggestions a
try. Second, I thought that I would be able to give it up in a
couple of months, and write a nice print-medium article about
how terrible this blogging thing was.

But within a few weeks, when I had most of the technical
issues mastered (though posting pictures, I must confess,
took a bit longer), I was really enjoying it. For a start, I found
that I was quite wrong about the dumbing down. What I had
not understood, before I actually experimented, was just how
important the 'links' on a blog were – and how they gave a
blog a distinct advantage over even the most learned article
in the most upmarket broadsheet. Imagine, for example,
that you want to refer in a newspaper to a newly discovered
poem of the Greek poetess Sappho, or to the *Res Gestae* of the
Roman emperor Augustus (an autobiographical account of his
reign, preserved by being carved into a Roman temple wall
in Ankara). The chances are you will not be able to. Only a
few of your readers will know what you are talking about, and
you won't have the space to explain it to the others. In a blog
it is different. You can put in a link not only to background
information, but to the whole text in Latin, Greek or English,
if you want to. Far from dumbing down, this was raising the

game of journalism. For the first time, I found I could refer casually to all sorts of aspects of my own academic specialism without excluding the vast majority of potential readers. To borrow a phrase from Sarah Boxer in the *New York Review of Books*, giving your readers a link is even better than giving them footnotes; it's more like giving them '3-D glasses'.

Then I quickly found the pleasure of using the blog to give some glimpse, from the inside, of what academic life is like – and, even more to the point, to dispel a few of the myths about our long holidays, the useless topics of our research or (in Oxford and Cambridge especially) the socially biased techniques we use to select our students. It was good to find, for example, that some sixth-formers were reading *my* account of what an interview for admission to my college might be like, rather than – or, at least, as well as – all those scare stories about the ridiculous questions we are rumoured to ask just to trip up the state school kids. On occasion, too, it was satisfying to right a few classical wrongs. Every classicist knows the frustration of reading the media hype over a range of non-discoveries: 'Cleopatra was not beautiful – shock'; 'Cave of Romulus discovered'; 'Bust of Julius Caesar dragged from river'; 'Socrates may have been gay'. I soon found that the blog was a place where I could respond to these travesties, and that the outside world just occasionally took notice. In fact, my responses were all the better and more powerful, not the worse, for being instant and a bit off the cuff. Another fear assuaged.

But perhaps the most positive thing for me was the interaction that began to develop with those who commented on my posts. *The Times* Online site, where *A Don's Life* is based, gives the blogger free rein to edit, publish or ignore the comments that are submitted. I decided very early on not to

exercise that power any more than was absolutely necessary.
I aimed to publish all the comments I received, unedited,
except for those that might be actionable, were trying to
sell something, were grossly irrelevant, or were personal
attacks on fellow commenters (personal attacks on me were,
I thought, within the rules). Even so, I started off very wary
of commenters as a breed. I had by now taken a look at other
blogs and had observed the rants and aggression directed
towards the blogger, as if the main pleasure of contributing
was to prove the blogger not only wrong but stupid. There was
something akin, I reflected, to the rhetorical style adopted by
callers to radio phone-in programmes.

The truth is that I have suffered a little bit of that. Every
now and then, when I have posted on a classical subject,
someone will write in with oozing disdain or outright insult to
put me right (often quite wrongly!) on the topic in hand. 'The
writer is a moron', as one person succinctly objected to one
post. I can occasionally find myself thinking, 'Hang on, who's
the Professor of Classics around here?'

But for the most part the comments and objections have
been witty, learned, entertaining, informative, sometimes
moving and occasionally multi-lingual or even in verse.
The commenters are, it turns out (for I have, by now, met or
corresponded with a good number of them), a far-flung crowd
– posting not only from Britain and the USA, but China,
Swaziland, India, France and Germany (to name only a few).
They include academics, museum curators, students, writers,
teachers, lawyers, journalists, musicians, retired tax inspectors,
health professionals, an ex-cabinet minister and (so I strongly
suspect) some of my own family in thinly veiled disguise. And
contrary to the image of the web as being a young person's
medium, many of them are my age (that's mid 50s) or older.

True, a *TLS* blog may not be the obvious first hit for the under 20s, but the age range is none the less reassuring.

Over the last few years there have been all kinds of articles on the web, and in print, about the role of blogging in politics and culture in general – from the contribution of the 'Baghdad Blogger', who posted his own view from the front line during the Iraq war, to that of the blogging detective 'Night Jack', the winner of the first George Orwell Blogging Prize for his posts about the reality of front line policing in Britain. (As I write, the future of Night Jack's blog, and of his career, remains in the balance, his anonymity having recently been broken by *The Times*.) Blogging has changed the shape and movement of political information and protest all over the world.

Even among academics, it has been the subject of some intense debate. Not simply, to blog or not to blog? But what to blog about and what authority should blogs have? Does a blog count, in academic terms, as a publication? Is it wise for disgruntled doctoral students looking for their first university post to blog about the humiliations of the job market? Probably not. But is it wise for doctoral students looking for an academic job to blog *at all*? Not according to 'Ivan Tribble', an American academic writing pseudonymously in the *Chronicle of Higher Education* some years ago. He had looked up the blogs of three young candidates for a job at his own university, and what he found played a major part in their not being hired ('… the site quickly revealed that the true passion of said blogger's life was not academe at all, but the minutiae of software systems, server hardware and other tech exotica'). I should say at this point that, although I have not always taken my own university's side in my blog, and although occasionally my posts have stimulated not wholly favourable publicity (see p. 39), there has been no attempt at all to stop me posting as I want. But then Cambridge is a place where academic freedom still means something.

Despite all this serious discussion, there has been very little interest in what seems to me one of the simplest satisfactions of blogging. Thanks to various 'tracking facilities', bloggers can know much more about who is reading them than any writer in a print newspaper or magazine. That is to say, I may write an editorial piece for a paper, but I have no idea how many of the tens of thousands who buy the paper actually read my piece, or for that matter how many start to read it but give up after the first paragraph. With the blog, using a clever service called Google Analytics, I can easily discover how many people click on a post (my top score is 80,000 for '10 things you thought you knew about the Romans … but didn't' (p. 139) – good, though not stratospheric, in comparative blog terms, but some way beyond the readership for anything else I've ever written). And I can also get an idea of just how much of the blog people read, because Analytics also registers their length of stay on the site. I'm currently averaging just over two and a half minutes a visit, which (given that the average must include a number of mis-hits, leaving the site in seconds) means that many of the posts are being read pretty thoroughly, from beginning to end.

Analytics can tell you even more about your readership. Happily, given my aversion to surveillance (see p. 6), it does not identify individual readers. But it does register the country from which they hit your blog. The readers in general are even further flung than the commenters. In 2008 I know that they came from 198 different nations of the world: more than half, it is true, from Britain and the USA, but plenty of hits also from most of the countries of Europe, plus Israel, India, South Africa, Japan, Brazil, Hong Kong and Singapore. Further down the list came, for example, China, Russia, Argentina, United

Arab Emirates, Estonia, Egypt, Pakistan, Lebanon, Kenya and Nepal – until you reached just single figures for Papua New Guinea, Kyrgyzstan, El Salvador, the Falklands, the Vatican and Benin, with finally just a solitary strike each for Somalia, Liechtenstein and American Samoa (though that one did stay on the site for ten minutes).

Even more intriguing is the information on what the punters had typed into Google to arrive at *A Don's Life*. Some sad tales of disappointment lurk just under the surface of this data. I do not for one moment imagine that the several hundred (10-year-old boys?) who typed 'pissing' into Google expected to arrive at my post on 'Pissing in the Pyramids' (p. 71). And I strongly suspect that the hundreds who every year type in 'Where is your spleen' have just returned from a visit to the doctor (and a spleen-related diagnosis). They are not likely to be satisfied with my 'Where is your spleen?' post – which was really about Classics undergraduates not being able to mark Athens or Sparta on a map.

So why the book? Blogs-into-books have had their critics. Thomas Jones once attacked the whole enterprise in the *London Review of Books*:

'Books and blogs,' he wrote, 'if they're doing their jobs properly, are as different as two kinds of published text can be. For one thing, creating a book takes many months … A blogger can have an unedited post up on the web and available to readers within minutes of the idea popping into his head. A blog is non-linear, always unfinished, ever open. It can be indefinitely added to, rewritten, cut from, commented on. But more than that, a blog should be dense with hyperlinks, sending the reader off into the blogosphere and the rest of the internet along a chain of endlessly forking paths. That may well sound like your idea of a nightmare, which is just one of the many reasons the internet isn't going to make books obsolete anytime soon.'

And he went on to describe one anthology of blog posts as 'an early contender for most pointless book of the year'.

There is a fair point here. Books and blogs are certainly very different. *It's A Don's Life* in book form is similar to, but not the same as, *A Don's Life* the blog. There have been losses in the metamorphosis – particularly in the chains of links that lie behind the blog text (in fact, those posts most dependant on 'linkage' have not been included). But there have, I believe, been gains, too – particularly in the material form of the book itself. Here you can browse more easily, and flip from one post to another, backwards and forwards. The book is also a convenient and portable commodity. No one I know reads their laptop on the Underground, in bed or in the loo.

So here we have *A Don's Life* for the journey to work, for going to sleep – or for the smallest room in the house.

Acknowledgements

This little book would not have been possible without Peter Stothard, who first suggested I do the blog, and the online team at *The Times* and *TLS* (especially Michael Caines, Lucy Dallas, Dan Leonard, Toby Lichtig, Michael Moran, Tom Whitwell and Rose Wild).

My family – Robin Cormack ('the husband'), Zoe and Raphael – has pointed me in all kinds of good blogging directions, and tolerated the laptop on the kitchen table with remarkably good grace. My colleagues at Cambridge have been supportive of a blogging don in their midst, and have cheerfully weathered the occasional controversies that have arisen. Thanks go especially to Greg Hayman for getting me out of one or two scrapes.

Making the book of the blog would have been impossible without the help in Cambridge of the wonderful Debbie Whittaker (who not only has sharper eyes than I have, but also entered into the true spirit of the project). The people at Profile have been as fun to work with as ever: Claire Beaumont, Peter Carson (whose idea the book was – but don't blame him), Penny Daniel, Andrew Franklin, Ruth Killick and Valentina Zanca. Thank you all.